Lisa,

Breathing Fire is filled
with the magic of my
angel cat, Star, so
don't be surprised if
you hear her purring as
you turn the pages.

With love,

Chris Davis

Breathing Fire

How a Knight From a Mythical Kingdom Awakened Me From a Spell

WRITTEN AND ILLUSTRATED BY CHRISTINE DAVIS

Breathing Fire

Lighthearted Press Inc.
P.O. Box 90125
Portland, OR 97290
503-786-3085 phone
503-786-0315 fax
www.lightheartedpress.com

Library of Congress Control Number: 2013951738

ISBN: 978-0-9659225-9-3 (hardcover)
ISBN: 978-0-9659225-8-6 (digital)

Printed in China

10 9 8 7 6 5 4 3 2 1

For Mom

Breathing Fire

Acknowledgments   *vii*
From the Author   *ix*

Part One: Beyond Here There Be Dragons
Merlin   2
A Quantum Change   4
A Little Girl's Plea for Help   6
Had I Been Here Before?   8
An Unexpected Miracle   9
The Call of the Blade   13
Body and Soul Reunited   14
A Spine Healed   15
These Can't Be My Clothes   16
The Seat Filler   18
A New York Girl in a Sword-Fighting Class   19
Calling Home My Sword   22
Surrender   29

Part Two: Living with Childhood Abuse in Your Past
Waiting for the Mother Ship   34
The Highly Sensitive Person   35
How to Keep Justifiable Rage Hidden   36
When in Doubt, Run   41
Martha, My Forever Dog   43
How to Fake Forgiveness   46

Part Three: The Women, the Men, and Christmas Eve
First Came the Women   50
Then Came the Men   52
The Return of Merlin   57
Becoming Fearless   59
Run Toward the Roar   60
Christmas Eve: The Night the Magic Ended   61

Part Four: The Magical Brain
Can We Consciously Change Our Brain?   70
Neuroplasticity   71
Where Did My Pain Go?   72
It's a Wonderful Life   73

Part Five: The Seven Gifts
Honor Where You Are   76
Seek Help When You Need It   78
Practice Giveaway   79
Surrender to Your Journey   80
Be Forgiving   82
What You Tolerate, You Teach   85
Laugh Often   86

Part Six: Coming Home
A Safe Haven   90
Why Arthur?   91
Home at Last   93
Watership Down   94

Epilogue   97

Notes   *101*

Acknowledgments

I could never have brought this book to life without the many special people who joined me on my journey, offering their open hearts and loving hands to my project. While it is impossible to mention them all, there are a few individuals I would like to acknowledge.

To my friend, Connie Bowen, for her unwavering honesty, encouragement, and passion. Thank you for always picking up the phone, even when you knew I was the one calling.

To the three earth angels, whose gifts of love provided a guiding light on Christmas Eve 2012: Judy Ditfurth, for helping me find my path; Jim Zeumer, my younger brother, for leading me back to my sword; Kathleen Otto, for returning me to the mystery.

To my older brother, Bob Zeumer, for filling in some of the gaps from my childhood and assuring me I didn't sleep in a box on the fire escape. To Michael Davis, my former husband, for teaching me how to use a symbolic shield. To my neighbors, Paula and Don Wolkerstorfer, for your friendship and support. To kindred spirits Kathleen Verigin and Layla Morgan Wilde, for being priestesses in my life.

To Peggy Laskoski, whose thoughtful input and editorial genius brought grace to my writing. Thank you for dancing with my dragons . . . and teaching them proper punctuation.

To Dr. William Miller, for helping me understand epiphanies. I will always be grateful for your kindness.

To Eric Kwang, for leaving a little memento of my extraordinary year on English soil.

To the many courageous women who came to me with their stories and urged me to write this book. And to the wise and gentle men who found me on my travels and gifted me with their perspective, bringing balance to my words.

To my angel cat, Star, who sprawled on the desk as I wrote this book, refusing to give in to her cancer. Thank you for staying as long as you could, sweet girl.

And finally—

To everyone connected with the show *Merlin*. Thank you for creating a world so enchanting I stepped eagerly into your kingdom and lost myself in the magic.

There is one cast member I would like to thank individually. To Bradley James, whose brilliant performance as Arthur released me from my childhood dragons and brought Clarity, my sword, back to my hand. I would like to share this magical blade with you. I realize the last thing you need is another sword, but you don't have *this* sword, Bradley. Clarity is wise—much more so than the woman who wields her. Should you ever need her counsel or care, she will always be here for you.

From the Author

At least once in life, a person should commit both heart and soul to doing something entirely on faith.

If you decide to do this, know that some people may not understand your journey. They may gently try to guide you back to the road you previously traveled. A few may kindly ask if you've been under a lot of stress lately and offer the name of a qualified therapist. Others may flat out call you crazy and run screaming in the opposite direction in case whatever has infected you is contagious.

The people who remain are your soul friends—those who are meant to accompany you on your odyssey. Your soul friends will share your vision, for they can see the wondrous path that is calling to you. And if part of that path becomes shrouded in mist, they will, nevertheless, stand by your side and cheer you on as you cross the finish line.

This is the story of my wild and unexpected journey of faith. It began with a television show that connected me to a mythical kingdom, where a faraway prince was waiting to come to my rescue. I had no idea I needed to be rescued. I was born and raised in New York City and never thought of myself as the damsel-in-distress type! The prince, however, was very wise and knew sometimes even a stubborn, independent, big-city girl can use a little help.

Many other people—some old friends, some new—joined me along the way. Each gifted me with something precious that ultimately found a place in my story.

From the beginning, I knew a dragon was destined to keep me company on my travels. The dragon would be both the one breathing fire behind me, ready to devour me whole, and the one flying beside me, keeping me on course.

And then there was Clarity—my sword. I didn't begin the year with a sword in my hand. Clarity was a gift of my journey, a reminder that faith often brings its own rewards. She was there by my side, when my travels brought me home.

Over the past year, I often thought of Noah building a vessel large enough to hold two of every species. They would need to survive forty days and nights of rain so they could repopulate the flooded earth when the water receded. There were those who ridiculed the building of the ark. But Noah was guided by something greater than any of them could understand—a sense of purpose. He had been given a sacred mission, and he intended to carry it out.

I do not liken myself to Noah, but I do understand the power of purpose. From the beginning of my adventure, I knew I was meant to write this story and share it with others. I didn't know how the story would end because it unfolded as I continued down my path. It has left me transformed—touched by something unimaginably glorious. I hope my words have done the story justice, but I fear no words can ever capture the feeling of being held in the arms of pure and utter bliss. How could mere words ever describe what it's like to feel one with everything in the Universe? Nevertheless, I was told to pass my story on, and that is what I've tried to do here.

I would like to emphasize that I am not a medical or mental health professional. If any of the physiological, psychological, emotional, or spiritual experiences I have shared sound intriguing, I suggest you seek advice from a qualified expert who can advise if this is the right path for you.

If you have traveled through the stars, you know those journeys are never a straight line. You may rise on the currents and fall when your wings are tired. You may go forward in time or back to a past that has memories waiting to be revisited. Such is the case with my journey. Those of you who enjoy wandering off the beaten path will feel at home with my travels. If, however, you prefer taking the shortest route to the final destination, I ask for your patience with my meanderings.

With love,

Chris

It is said that old world cartographers used to write Beyond Here There Be Dragons where the known territory ended on their maps. This was to alert ships they were about to enter uncharted and dangerous waters.

A version of these words was found only once on a sixteenth century globe, but their poetry has lingered. Had there been a map of my life, Beyond Here There Be Dragons would have been painted in bold lettering across its length, a warning to pay attention to the unexpected and miraculous odyssey that began for me in the summer of 2012.

Part One

Beyond Here There Be Dragons

"No, I would not want to live in a world without
dragons, as I would not want to live in a world
without magic, for that is a world without
mystery, and that is a world without faith."
—R.A. Salvatore (Streams of Silver)[1]

Merlin

EVERY JOURNEY HAS STEPS THAT can't be hurried, skipped, or rearranged.

My journey began one morning when I was at my desk paying the household bills. The statement from the cable company sat on top of the stack. Every month, I looked at this bill and wondered if I could continue justifying the high cost of my cable package, given how little time I had for watching television. I decided the moment had come. If I couldn't find at least one new show that would keep me enthralled, I'd call the cable folks and scale back on my channels.

The remote was nearby, so I brought up the guide and peeked at the upcoming programming. I scanned so quickly it all went by in a blur, as if I was spinning a wheel on a game show, hoping to win the trip to Maui. All I wanted was a television experience that would touch my heart and set my soul on fire. Was that too much to ask for?

Suddenly, I saw something. It was a single word—*Merlin*. Why had I never seen this show before? The name conjured up many wondrous images: a mystical sword being pulled from a stone, heroic King Arthur ruling over the Kingdom of Camelot, chivalrous knights riding out on perilous adventures, forbidden passions threatening to tear the kingdom apart, and the wizard, Merlin, under whose guidance all of this would unfold.

It looked like they were going to run the first two seasons of the show. I didn't know *Merlin* had already aired for four seasons. I decided to record all twenty-six episodes, and several days later, stepped with great anticipation into Camelot.

It didn't take long to realize that I loved *Merlin*! The premise of the show was delightful, the writing was excellent, the actors were engaging, and the music was enchanting. What wasn't to like?

Over the next week, I made my way through the first twenty episodes. In this version of Camelot, magic is forbidden and sorcerers are put to death, a law strictly upheld by the king, Uther Pendragon. The young wizard, Merlin, arrives in Camelot and is given the position of servant to the king's son, Prince Arthur. Even though Merlin must keep his magic hidden from the prince he serves, a friendship forms between the two men. We meet Morgana, the king's ward, who lives in fear of her prophetic dreams in a land where such gifts usually result in a swift execution. And we are introduced to Guinevere, the blacksmith's daughter, whose disinterest in Arthur softens as a romance begins to blossom between her and the prince.

Then I came to episode twenty-one.

It was called "The Sins of the Father." In this episode, Arthur meets an enchantress who grants the prince his one wish—to see the mother who died in childbirth when he was born. His mother tells him she was unable to conceive, which meant there would be no heir to the throne upon the king's death. Arthur learns that his father consorted with a sorceress, who used magic to bring a son into the world. He is told the king knowingly sacrificed his wife to ensure the continuation of the Pendragon line. The birth of Arthur meant the death of his mother—a life for a life.

Learning his father kept the true circumstances of his birth a secret is a crushing blow to Arthur. He knows his father is responsible for his mother's death. He sees his father as a hypocrite, one who has executed people for possessing magical abilities, even though he used magic himself. The enraged prince rides back to the castle, throws open the door, and stands before his father.

From that moment on, my life would never be the same.

A Quantum Change

DR. WILLIAM MILLER IS EMERITUS Distinguished Professor of Psychology and Psychiatry at the University of New Mexico. He is the author of many scientific publications that reflect his interests in the treatment of addictions and the psychology of change. He and psychologist Janet C'de Baca became intrigued by a different type of change that some of the people they encountered had experienced—moments of inexplicable clarity and profound healing that came from out of the blue. When they placed a request in a local paper for people's stories of unexpected personal transformations, the response was overwhelming.

In their book, *Quantum Change: When Epiphanies and Sudden Insights Transform Ordinary Lives*,[2] the authors say that when a quantum change occurs in one's life, it is characterized by four elements:

◉ Vividness—individuals know that something remarkable has happened.

◉ Surprise—the experience is unexpected. The individual didn't "do" anything to prompt the transformation. It just happened.

◉ Benevolence—it is perceived as profoundly positive and beneficial.

◉ Permanence—individuals are changed forever.

It's difficult for a writer to admit she can't find words to describe an experience, yet how could mere words ever capture what happened to me as I watched the next few minutes of *Merlin*?

Barely able to contain the anger seething within him, Arthur confronts his father. "I know what you did to my mother."[3]

He rips the gauntlet from his arm and throws it to the ground, demanding the king pick it up. Then he draws his sword.

What follows is rage—visceral, unrelenting rage. Arthur's blade cuts savagely through the air. Out pours all the grief and heartbreak felt by this son who has been betrayed by his parent. He disarms his father, pins him back in his chair, and holds the sword at his neck.

"You have caused so much suffering and pain! I will put an end to that!"[4]

It is Merlin who rushes in, desperate to prevent a murder he knows the prince would never be able to live with. He lies to Arthur, convincing him it was the enchantress who had deceived him, not his father.

"Swear to me it isn't true! You are not responsible for my mother's death! Give me your word!"[5]

Arthur's words are hurled at his father. Uther swears he would never have hurt Arthur's mother, and his son believes him.

Arthur drops to the ground at the king's side and tearfully apologizes. "You are not to blame,"[6] his father says.

I had recorded *Merlin* on the downstairs television in the living room and also on the one upstairs in my bedroom. As it turned out, I was watching this episode on the TV in my bedroom, at about 9:00 p.m.

I don't know how it happened. I don't even remember it happening. One moment I was propped up on my pillows, watching Arthur tear the gauntlet from his arm, the ominous look in his eyes a hint of what was about to be unleashed. The next moment, I was standing on the other side of the bedroom, my fingernails stabbing into the palms of my clenched fists, listening to the agonizing screams that were erupting from my throat. I was engulfed in an inferno of unyielding, uncontrollable fury. Every tiny particle of space was saturated with my rage. It mirrored the rage I saw on the screen pouring forth from Arthur. Neither of us could be constrained.

I felt a hand reaching through the layers of my skin. It was searching for something horrific that had been lurking deep within me. The hand probed all the nooks and crannies of my soul until it found what it was looking for.

A terrifying bellow exploded like thunder within my body. A monster was awakened, furious that its long hibernation had been disturbed. It reared its beastly head and roared with all the ferocity it could muster. The creature knew it was about to be forced from its hiding place.

And it was angry.

A Little Girl's Plea for Help

THE FOLLOWING IS EXCERPTED FROM a piece I wrote in 1993 called *Fragments*. It was about years of sexual and psychological abuse I endured as a child at the hands of my father.

The Little Girl

Once upon a time a little girl
was born into the world.
From the moment she opened her eyes
she knew something was wrong.
She knew there had been a mistake,
and the wrong mother and father
had come to take her home.

But it was too late.

So home she went, this magical bundle
in the arms of two people who would
never know, and never care,
how precious the gift they carried was.

As time went by, the little girl
came to know that she was
living in a nightmare.

She realized a child was not
safe in the house in which she lived.

So the little girl said,
"I must go away now. I must hide."

But the little girl was very smart.

"How do I disappear," she wondered,
"and not be missed?"

One night, she prayed to the stars
in the night sky for guidance.
The next day her prayers were answered.
In her place was a grown-up,
living inside her little girl shell.

The grown-up did not know that she
had once been a little child.
The grown-up did not know she had
been summoned by a child
afraid for her life.

To the rest of the world,
this grown-up looked like the child
she had always been.

But inside, the child who had
never laughed, never played,

never been carefree,
never been a child,
had vanished.

The grown-up did what grown-ups do.
She assessed the situation.

She put on her armor
and took up her sword.

I must be ready to protect myself
from all of them
for as long as I have to

Even forever.

Had I Been Here Before?

TWO YEARS AFTER I WROTE those words, I discovered a book called *Soul Retrieval: Mending the Fragmented Self,*[7] by Sandra Ingerman. The author is a licensed Marriage and Family Therapist, as well as a board certified expert on traumatic stress. In her book, she describes an ancient shamanic healing ritual used to find—and bring home—lost parts of a person's soul that have fled the body in order to survive a past traumatic event.

I thought about the part of me that had abandoned my body as a child in order to survive my father's abuse. Could a soul retrieval help bring that little girl back? I decided to meet with a local shaman and have the ritual performed. I didn't tell him anything about my past. He recorded his findings when he was done, so we could discuss what he had discovered on his journey.

The shaman told me he had encountered several lost parts of my soul, but he was most intrigued by the piece that was present at my birth. It clearly did not want to be here. He said sometimes this will show up in a child as illness, such as asthma or other breathing issues. I told the shaman I had never been a sickly baby, but that hadn't been the case for my older sister, Pamela, who died when she was just a few weeks old.

"I was the next baby," I said.

There was the sound of a large intake of breath.

"You were also the first baby," whispered the shaman.

"What do you mean?" I asked.

He looked straight into my eyes. "That first girl was also you."

As soon as he spoke those words, I felt a shiver down to my core. Could this be true? Had I been born into this family once before?

"Why do you think I was sent back?" I asked.

"Perhaps," he offered, "a higher power said you must go back. There was work to be done within this family and it was time for it to be completed."

Perhaps. Or maybe I was ready to come back.

An Unexpected Miracle

WHEN THE *MERLIN* EPISODE ENDED, I replayed those last few moments again . . . and again . . . and again. Each time I saw Arthur's anguished face I felt the monster heaving within me. Its barbed claws latched onto my soul as it clung desperately to its lair. But this was a battle it could not win. The beast let out one final, agonizing bellow. Then it was forcibly ripped from my body and thrown into the furious particles agitating around me. The collision of my inner rage with my outer rage resulted in an explosion so catastrophic I should have been decimated in the blast. But I wasn't.

Instead, I held my ground.

Silence.

How much time had gone by? A second? A minute? A lifetime?

I wasn't breathing.

Take a breath, Chris.

I peered into the space before me. I was facing the shadowy corner of the room that held my canopy bed. My hands were tightly wrapped around one of the bedposts. I must have shaken it violently, because the top boards connecting the four posts had come apart and were dangling precariously over the mattress.

Take a breath, Chris.

I pulled my hands from the bedpost and slowly turned around. The recording of *Merlin* had ended. It was eerily quiet. The glow from the television lit the room, but everything seemed out of focus. I needed to sit down. Ever so gently, I dropped to the floor and steadied my back against the bed. Then I began to breathe.

I just breathed.

With each cleansing breath, I felt something rising within me. It was JOY. In that moment, I knew somehow, some way—from across the globe—a character in a television show had released a lifetime of pent-up rage buried deep in my soul. I may have been unable to scream at my father for his unspeakable abuse, but Arthur was not so encumbered. When he disarmed the king and held the blade to his neck, I saw it as my father who had been disarmed by the prince. It was my father whose reign of terror had been stopped by Arthur's sword. It was my father who was finally being held accountable for his crimes.

This is the only version of Camelot I have ever seen in which Arthur is raised by his father. Had that not been the premise of the show, this episode would never have occurred and I would still be a prisoner of my toxic anger.

I had been given an extraordinary gift—the gift of clarity. When I watched Arthur succumb to his father at the end of that scene, I knew that I would never succumb to my father again. That part of my journey was over. In an instant, my life-story had been rewritten, a process that would leave my brain rewired and my perception of the world profoundly altered.

I was now a completely different person. I had been transformed by Arthur Pendragon of Camelot and by a storyline that contained the exact elements I needed to release me from my past and make me whole again.

But it wasn't just about the character of Arthur or the perfectly written script.

It was about the sword.

I had watched twenty previous episodes of *Merlin*, each filled with characters wielding swords, yet I hadn't been touched by their presence. They were part of the wardrobe, like the boots and capes.

Suddenly, my hand was reaching into the mist, searching for the sword that was waiting for me to call it back home. I felt it being offered, as

Excalibur had been presented to Arthur by the Lady of the Lake. Accepting this sword meant I must carry it with wisdom and compassion. It would symbolize freedom from my haunted past and lead me to a future brimming with possibilities.

The rage, the sword, and the son succumbing to the father became the three parts of this scene that would manifest a miracle in my life. I was freed from a demon that had held me captive ever since I was a child.

I knew I was no longer alone in my room. Standing next to me was a little girl, whose joyful giggles bubbled forth and filled the air around us. She reached up and tenderly put her tiny hand in mine. We had found each other again.

How often had I called to her throughout my lifetime, hoping she might come back to me? How many years had I longed to hear her laughter? Now I understood she had been waiting for the angry monster to leave, because only then would it be safe to return. There would be no un-finished business with my father. It happened in that one cataclysmic moment. As soon as my rage exploded into nothingness, my little girl came home.

It was the combination of the actor's brilliant portrayal of a child deceived and the sword pointing at his father's neck that brought me to this place. Without knowing he had done so, a prince from a faraway kingdom had not only changed my life, he had saved it.

Words from a card I had seen danced inside my heart: "They asked the little girl what do you want to do with your life . . . and she said EVERY-THING!"

The Call of the Blade

I REMEMBER ALL TOO WELL my first introduction to a blade. I was about three years old, and my mother had been pushing one of my friends on a metal swing in the park. I stood up just in time for the swing to come back and hit me hard in the forehead. The resulting goose-egg demanded a quick lancing. I was rushed to the doctor's office where a nurse held down my arms, my mother held down my legs, and the doctor sliced open my head.

That experience left me with a healthy fear of knives. Even being near them in the kitchen was uncomfortable.

Something changed for me in 2002 when I saw Eowyn wield a sword in the second part of the *Lord of the Rings* trilogy—*The Two Towers*. As with *Merlin*, I had watched hours of swordplay in the first part of the trilogy without sensing any connection to the blade. It wasn't until I saw the sword held defiantly in a woman's hand that my heart began beating wildly. I left the theater knowing somewhere out there, in time and space, I once held a sword.

This led me to a cutlery store in the mall. Oddly enough, the name of the store was Excalibur. I was eager to have the salesman select a sword from the wall of weapons and present it to me like a firstborn child. I quickly accepted Glamdring, the sword that had belonged to the wizard, Gandalf, into my waiting arms. I waved it around with great fanfare and then paused with excitement as I held it majestically over my head. I noticed the salesman had gone a bit pale. He politely asked me to lower the sword so no one would get hurt. Then he muttered something about liability issues.

I looked at a young man standing a bit further down behind the counter and said, "I'll bet it's thrilling for you to be around all these weapons!"

"Not really," he answered. Then he pointed to a wooden block filled with delicate kitchen knives. "That's what I'm holding out for. I want to be a pastry chef."

What was wrong with this picture?

After that day, I put the sword idea out of my head. It never crossed my mind again until ten years later when I saw *Merlin*.

Body and Soul Reunited

THE IMPACT OF KNOWING I was free from my past was immediate—and it was powerful!

I felt like I had been dropped into my body like Dorothy's house had been dropped into Oz. And just like Dorothy, when I looked out upon my new world everything was in glorious, vibrant color.

I moved beyond feeling joyful. I was euphoric.

Sleep became impossible as my energy level skyrocketed. I began prowling through my home at night, unnerved by primal feelings I couldn't explain. The wild creature within me had returned. I felt like a feral animal set free from a cage. Many a night, I found myself sprawled on the bedroom rug at two o'clock in the morning, digging my nails into the carpet like claws on a log.

My eating habits also changed. I'd been a vegetarian for thirty years, but I knew there was room for improvement in my diet. I was consuming too many milk and sugar products. After watching *Merlin*, my desire for most sweets and dairy items came to a screeching halt. They simply didn't appeal to me anymore.

For much of my life, I struggled with low blood sugar. This meant eating a small meal every few hours to prevent myself from becoming light-headed. I had passed out in some very fine places on both sides of the country. Without giving it any thought, I stopped those frequent meals and only went into the kitchen when I felt hungry. This turned out to be less often than I ever would have expected. I never experienced another low blood sugar episode.

The change in my eating habits led to rapid weight loss. My body responded enthusiastically to not being stuffed with food. I lost thirty pounds in three months! As the weight fell off, I found myself moving differently through space. It was exhilarating to know that the footprint I was leaving on the earth was not as deep as it had been before. I felt lighter, and my steps were quicker. I wondered if this was how my little cat, Star, felt when she raced through my home like a beam of light bouncing off the walls.

A Spine Healed

I HAD ONE OTHER PHYSIOLOGICAL problem that had caused me no end of grief and pain—my spine. I was born with an anomaly that led to two spine surgeries, but new spinal problems were continually showing up. My car could drive itself to the physical therapist's office. I owned enough PT equipment to start my own practice. My neck traction device was a dear friend.

In 2008 I watched the presidential election results with my left leg up on pillows. I didn't know it at the time, but the muscles running from the hip to the knee had collapsed, leaving my left knee cap facing the right leg. I was able to avoid surgery, but spent the first half of 2009 in physical therapy getting the knee back in working order.

In 2011 I sat down to illustrate my book, *Forever Paws*, and knew I was in trouble. My lower spine had actually shifted forward, a condition called spondylolisthesis. I had no idea if I would be able to find a position that would allow me to hover over the artwork for several months. Thankfully, some strategically placed pillows beneath my feet and a back brace (hefty enough for a sumo wrestler) allowed me to complete the illustrations.

I began 2012 with yet another spinal issue. Hoping to avoid the surgeon's blade, I found my way to Karen, a caring massage therapist, whose gifted hands proved to be a life saver. If I moved carefully, continued my regular gym routine, and didn't do anything idiotic, I might just make it through the year without any more problems.

Then I watched *Merlin*. I was thrown powerfully back into my body. I'll never be able to say for certain what happened, but from that moment on, I never had another problem with my spine. Was it a miracle? Was it a coincidence? Or was it possible my rewired brain accepted my transformation into someone who didn't have a spinal problem?

These Can't Be My Clothes

IN ADDITION TO ALL OF the physical changes, another surprising issue cropped up. It was my clothing. It's not uncommon for adult female survivors of childhood abuse to dress in loose-fitting apparel. Most of my life had been spent wearing clothes that could have been designed by a tentmaker.

Shortly after watching *Merlin*, I began looking at the items in my closet through the eyes of an alien visiting from another planet. "These must be what the female earthlings wear," I thought. "Perhaps garments for an older, larger humanoid."

This new view of my clothing was eye-opening. My closet emanated a sadness I never noticed before. Looking at these oversized clothes made me realize just how disconnected from my body I had been. I saw myself as a doll in a toy store, sitting in a box on a shelf. The name on my box was printed in bold letters. It said **Broken Child**. Below the name were the words: Shapeless garments for all occasions included. Head comes tilted in a downward position. This lifelike doll cries real tears. Therapist doll sold separately.

I laughed when I wrote that line about the therapist doll, until I realized that the word *therapist* breaks down into *the rapist*. I wondered if this was accidental. I suspected it wasn't.

Now that the connection to my past was severed, the costumes I assembled for the years I lived as a broken child no longer had a place in my wardrobe. Within a few months, I gave away most of my clothing and began buying outfits for a younger, female humanoid . . . with curves.

It became clear that I had come back to the body I deserted as a child. I suspected, however, something astonishing had happened. Instead of returning at my current age, the Universe—in a gesture of supreme generosity—brought me back with the body, mind, spirit, and desires of a much younger woman. I was being given a chance to relive a part of my life that had been lost due to the heartbreak and suffering from my youth.

Now what?

I remember the day I told this story to a friend.

"Kathleen," I said, "I believe I've gone back to a younger age."

"Just like Merlin," she replied.

Of course! In some versions of the Camelot story, Merlin doesn't age as time moves forward. Instead, he becomes younger. Could this be part of the strange connection that had drawn me to the television show?

The Seat Filler

WITH THE OVER-SIZED CLOTHING GONE from my closet, and my passion for living at an all-time high, I realized one more gift had come my way the night I experienced my quantum change. I was no longer a seat-filler.

Many years ago, I heard about people who are hired as seat-fillers at televised events. A seat-filler takes the chair of a celebrity in case he or she is late or has to leave temporarily, so the space won't be empty on television. It was a sad day when I realized an awful truth. I had become a seat-filler in my own life, holding the space until the important person came along. I was not participating in my life—I was simply observing it. I had allowed my world to become small, its boundaries tight around me. The wonders of the Universe might beckon to me, but they would always be just beyond my grasp.

The words of Dr. Clarissa Pinkola Estés, author of *Women Who Run with the Wolves*,[8] haunted me: "Women are trained to remain contained."

When the shaman performed my soul retrieval, he asked if there were any creatures wanting to present themselves as power animals for me. These animals would offer their wisdom, guidance, and protection. They would help me to understand and fulfill the divine purpose for my life. Three animals came forward, one of which was the hawk—a mystical, visionary bird whose realm is the sky. He is known as the messenger. If *hawk* is your totem, pay attention, for he has much to tell you.

In the 1967 movie *Camelot*, the wizard, Merlin, gives King Arthur the opportunity to experience life as a hawk. As the king soars through the skies, Merlin calls to him and asks what he knows as a hawk that he doesn't know as Arthur. Arthur realizes that from above he can see the forests, lakes, and castles, but he can't see any edges. Boundaries can only be seen by the human beings who establish them, as they walk the earth.

For far too long, my power animal's wisdom could not find its way to my heart. He had much to say, but I was unable to hear him. Hawk and I have finally become friends. When I soar through the starry skies, hawk often joins me in flight. He navigates the winds better than I, but I'm learning. He is patient, my hawk, and for that, I am grateful. When I watch him fly away, I now hear his message with perfect clarity. "There are no boundaries," he cries, "unless you choose to accept them!"

I have stepped into my confidence. With unwavering conviction, I have claimed my seat, and lo and behold, it sits before a round table. A sword rests at my side, for swords are welcome here. I traveled for many years before coming to this hallowed place. The road was long and winding, but I was always destined to arrive.

A New York Girl in a Sword-Fighting Class

I THOUGHT ABOUT SWORDS CONSTANTLY after the *Merlin* experience. Somewhere out there in the Universe lived a sword that was destined for my hand. We were being drawn to each other like partners coming together for a cosmic dance.

I had a crystal clear vision of what my sword would look like. I also knew what her name would be. Yes, my sword was definitely feminine. Everything else was a mystery. Since I knew nothing at all about blades, it seemed the next leg of my journey would involve training. It was time for sword-fighting instruction.

I will never forget the first day I showed up for sword class. I sat in my car reading the bumper stickers on the other vehicles: "Real men play with their swords" and "My other ride is a pirate ship."

I had found my people!

I walked into the large room and looked around. One long wall was mirrored from floor to ceiling. The rest of the room was covered in armor and swords of every shape and size. It looked like ballet class—with weapons.

This particular lesson was on the fundamentals of holding a sword and shield. I watched the men peruse the blades and confidently grab the one of their choice. You could almost see them reverting back to little boys, to a time when holding a toy sword was as natural as breathing.

The instructor put a sword in my hand. I asked the same question I would often hear women ask when they first picked up a sword: "How do I hold it?" I don't ever recall hearing a man ask that question, even men who were attending their first sword class. They didn't care.

So I stood there, in front of the mirror, holding my sword before me. Thanks to ten years of ballet lessons my feet were turned out in the wrong position. The lifelong disconnection from my body had robbed me of a sense of balance, something the instructor proved by lightly touching my shoulder and watching me fall over. When he put the shield in my other hand, I realized how puny and weak my arms were.

But none of this mattered to me, because holding a sword in my hand left me feeling perfectly and utterly complete. It was as if something that had been missing from my life was restored. It went beyond feeling ecstatic—it was more like remembering a feeling of unimaginable ecstasy from a long time ago. Perhaps I was doing everything wrong, but being here was right.

I learned something important about myself in this first class. Despite my instantaneous connection with the sword, there was very little warrior energy within me. I could muster up a mediocre version of it should an animal be in need, but if I had to defend myself, I was in trouble. I felt spineless. Perhaps those feelings had found their way to my vertebrae, joints, and muscles. No wonder I had needed two spine surgeries!

I looked at the men in the class and saw the conviction on their faces as they worked the swords and shields. They were focused, committed, and ready for battle. I wanted some of what they had. I knew I would never be a ten on the warrior-energy Richter scale, but I didn't want to be. If I could land somewhere around a four I'd be content.

During the last thirty minutes of the class, my arms grew weary. Both the sword and shield felt like they weighed twenty pounds each. Was it so wrong of me to hope the building had scheduled an unannounced fire drill and at any moment the alarm would go off?

It was time to put the weapons away for the night. I walked out to the car with a silly grin on my face. I'd had a great time in sword class. I thought about ways I might ramp up the warrior part of my personality. I also needed to work on my balance. Thankfully, I lived with two master teachers in this area—my fabulous felines. If anyone knows about balance, it's a cat.

In addition to working with the sword, I needed to learn how to fall correctly. This meant landing consciously so I could protect my vulnerable parts and not get injured. I remember the first time we did tumbling exercises in class. I wondered what my physical therapist would say if he could see my head tucked into my chest as I threw myself over onto the fall mats.

Despite my connection to the sword, it was clear that if I ever was to compete in a pageant, sword-fighting would not be my talent. I was more interested in the symbolism of the blade than using it as a weapon. However, the class had shown me that I needed to build up my strength. I elevated my workout routine at the gym and began using the weights I had at home. It turned out they were good for more than keeping my DVDs in place.

The weeks went by and I never had one tweak or twinge in my back. No combination of sword, shield, or armor caused me any trouble. I spoke with my friend, Connie, about the miraculous healing my spine had undergone.

"Your back has been forged in steel," she said, "just like your sword."

That took my breath away.

Calling Home My Sword

I SAW HER LONG BEFORE I held her. She had been resting for over a thousand years in a craggy boulder, which sat by the edge of a stream in a misty forest. She was partially cloaked in moss, her exposed parts left to darken over time. The trees had gathered around her in a circle, weaving a leafy canopy that kept her resting place a secret from all but the one who had placed her in the stone and the one to whom she called.

She called to me.

She had been calling to me since I was a little girl. I heard her whispering in my dreams, telling me our destinies were entwined long before either of us came into being. She was waiting for me to call her back home. Until our reunion, she would watch over me from the water's edge and follow my adventures from afar.

From the moment I saw Arthur disarm his father and hold him at the end of his blade, I knew the time had come to answer her call. I was ready to manifest this magical sword in my life.

It began with a simple sketch. I drew her as I had seen her in my visions:

- The pommel—the end of the sword that acts as a counterweight for balance—would be shaped like a spiral.

- The cross-guard—the part that is perpendicular to the blade and protects the hand—would be embedded with stars.

- The hilt—where you hold the sword between the pommel and the cross-guard—would be wrapped in the colors of water.

- The fuller—the groove that goes down the blade to help lighten the sword—would be etched with the words *ALWAYS FOLLOW YOUR HEART*.

I knew one other thing about my sword. Her name would be Clarity, because that was what had been given to me the night I watched the twenty-first episode of *Merlin*.

None of these points, however, have anything to do with the actual construction of the sword. For that, I turned to Grendel, the blacksmith from across the river who would bring her to life.

You may wonder how it was that I knew a blacksmith named Grendel. Once I began spending time with people who carried swords, finding my way to a blacksmith was easy. I remember the first time I drove to his forge. I showed him my simple sword illustration, explaining I wanted her to have an earthy quality. If I could have planted "sword seeds" and grown one in the garden I would have happily done that.

There were many blades in Grendel's workspace. I picked up several swords, looking for a perfect fit to use as a template. I was not creating a weapon for fighting—I was creating a symbolic sword that would be used for ceremony. I might not be swinging this sword in battle, but she still needed to feel right in my hand.

When it came time to leave, I realized Grendel didn't know about the journey that had led me to his forge. Suddenly, I wanted to share my story with him. He pulled over an empty, rusted, fifty-five gallon drum, sat down, and looked me straight in the eye. I stood about ten feet in front of him and began telling him of my great adventure. I told him about the show *Merlin*, and how Prince Arthur had disarmed his father with the sword. I cried as I shared what happened the night all my rage was released.

I spoke for a long time. Grendel never moved. He gave me his complete attention. When I was finished, I felt like I had participated in a sacred ceremony. This man was about to create something that had been calling to me my entire life. Perhaps, one day, this sword would bring inspiration and hope to others who felt a kinship with her.

When I left the forge, I knew in my heart that Grendel understood why I had come to him that day. He would make me the perfect sword.

I made several trips back and forth to Grendel's forge over the next few months. I never envisioned Clarity as an elegant sword, highly polished and fit for royalty. I knew she had a free-spirited nature—if she took to a body, she would run barefoot through the woods like a forest sprite, her feet covered in pine needles and dirt. When she could run no more, her body would explode into a million little stars that would float up to the heavens.

We decided to leave the pommel and cross-guard rough and partly blackened. It was Grendel who suggested rolling the pommel, like a lollipop, into the spiral shape. This made my inner child very happy.

The day came when Clarity was complete, and Grendel placed her in my hands. Together, we had brought this wondrous metal being to life. As I put her in the back seat of my car, I sensed I was in the presence of something divine. Was that emanating from the sword, or had a heavenly being joined us for the ride home? I had often envisioned Clarity being held by an angel. Perhaps a messenger from above was here to bless the next leg of our miraculous adventure.

When I got home, I carried Clarity into my office, which is the only room in my house that has a twenty-foot high ceiling. My wrap-around desk runs along two walls. It's covered with multiple computers, books, candles, painted rocks, and various other accoutrements that keep this writer happy.

On the other side of the room sits my piano. Long before I ever thought about writing, I played piano and sang. Throughout any given day, I go back and forth between the computer keyboard and the piano keyboard, typing words for books and playing notes for songs. The creative force comes from a mysterious place in my soul. This is where the writing fairy lives—the one who brings exactly the word I'm seeking for a song or story. There is powerful energy in this room.

I stood in the middle of the office and held Clarity in my hands. I took a moment to thank the Universe for bringing this beloved sword-sister into my life. I closed my eyes, offering myself to all the creativity and passion that had been infused into this space. It surrounded us like a glowing circle of light. I wrapped my fingers around the blue and green leathers that encircled Clarity's hilt and looked upward, tears filling my eyes. With one fluid movement, I thrust the sword toward the sky, piercing the light in such a way it fractured into a thousand brilliant beams that emanated from the point of Clarity's blade and filled the room around us.

In the middle of all that light something was revealed to me. Clarity carried within her the spirit of all the swords that had brought me to this moment: the one held by the adult I became when the child inside me fled; the one held by Eowyn in *The Lord of the Rings*; the sword of Gandalf that had captivated me in the cutlery store; and the one wielded by Arthur in the scene that would change the course of my life.

With that ceremony, I welcomed Clarity home.

There is a small rock garden on my hillside that holds the remains of my first forever dog, Martha. Many years ago, I had one of the rocks engraved with the word that best described Martha's enchanted nature. I placed Clarity by that rock and took some pictures. When I looked at the photos I saw a perfect composition—my mystical sword, Clarity, next to a rock bearing the word *MAGIC*.

I told people about Clarity long before I brought her home. When someone would ask if I was working on anything new, I'd mention the book I was writing about the wild and wonderful direction my life had taken. People were fascinated to hear how a character in a television show had released me from my haunted past, and how a sword was going to lead me into a new and magnificent future.

I decided I would offer Clarity to others who felt drawn to her. Some had been inspired by my story and were eager to sever the ties that kept them bound to their own painful past. Others were seeking protection and guidance, or sensed the need of a powerful ally in their life. A few people thought she might be skilled at cutting through red tape. Whatever the intention, I knew Clarity was ready to be of service.

When I only had the original sketch, I emailed it to interested people. When Clarity was completed, I sent the photo of her next to the *MAGIC* rock. They might not be able to hold her, but she had the ability to empower women nevertheless. I began to realize that even though Clarity and I had a joined destiny, there were times we were meant to work apart. I would let others know she was available. Deciding how best to connect would be between Clarity and those who felt called to her.

Clarity is now a part of my life. She is imbued with the reverence I feel for her, which is mighty, indeed. She rests on my desk, free of a scabbard. After all those years embedded in a stone, she enjoys the open air.

For many months, I wondered who it was that had placed Clarity in the stone over a thousand years ago. Was it a white-bearded wizard in long flowing robes? Was it a dispirited king, weary of wars that never came to completion? Was it a divine entity, preserving the blade for a coming warrior who would carry the sword into a new crusade?

One day I heard myself say the words, "It was I."

Could that be true? Did Clarity and I have a life together long before she came to this writer's hand in the year 2012? Had she and I fought together in countless wars, her blade catching the light of the setting sun as each day turned to darkness? When our battles came to an end, was it time for her to rest, while I continued on without her? "There is much for you to learn on your own," she said. "Stand me in a rock by the water's edge, so I can watch over you from afar. The trees will gather around me and keep my resting place a secret until we are meant to find each other again."

I did as Clarity asked and stepped into the future without her. Centuries passed until I came to the current lifetime. According to the shaman, I was terrified to be in this body knowing the difficult road I would be traveling. If he was correct, it took two attempts for me to come into my family and surrender to the work I needed to do. Until I could move through all my grief and rage, I would continue to be mired in my past.

And that is where I would have remained had it not been for the show *Merlin* and for Arthur Pendragon of Camelot. Why this character, in a single episode, was able to accomplish what a long line of highly qualified and well-intentioned therapists could not remains a mystery to me.

After the miraculous events that occurred when I watched *Merlin*, I knew I was meant to share my experience with others who had walked a similar path. I hoped it would embolden them by offering a way out of the darkness. And leading us into the light would be Clarity. If, in our past, I had wielded her to injure or kill, those fighting days were behind both of us now.

Clarity would come to my hand only to inspire. I would hold her for others who needed a champion. A space had been created where those who were hurt or broken could gather. We would share our stories and set our intentions to move beyond our sorrow. Perhaps, after all, I was that future warrior who would carry the sword in a new crusade.

As soon as I stepped into that place, Clarity came back to me. She had been waiting patiently, knowing that when it was time for her to return to my hand I would call her home.

Surrender

I THOUGHT ABOUT ALL THE changes that had happened to me in a short period of time. I was in better shape and was more energetic than I'd been in my twenties and thirties. The woman who looked back at me in the mirror was joyful, confident, and she finally carried a sword.

Most remarkable of all, I was suddenly more in touch with the physical side of my nature than I had ever been in my life. I finally understood all the women I'd seen at a pirate festival. Those women were in their power. They wore low-cut bustiers and skirts slit to the thigh. It didn't matter if they were size four, fourteen, or twenty-four— they flaunted whatever they had, loving themselves exactly as they were. It was intoxicating to be around women so self-assured. I understood how men would be captivated by them.

I've watched enough talk shows to know there are four areas in which women universally seek guidance: looking more youthful, feeling more energetic, losing excess weight, and reclaiming their sexual lives. I had graciously been given gifts that touched on each of these areas, and the gifts came with clear instructions—pass them on.

From the beginning of this extraordinary adventure, I knew somehow I was being guided. I continually heard I needed to trust that all was unfolding as it was meant to, in its own way and in its own time. I had been invited onto a magical tour bus. I didn't know where it came from, and I had no idea where it was going. I assumed I would be the tour director, or—perhaps—the bus driver. It became clear that I was not meant to be either. I was being gently, but firmly, told to take a seat in the passenger section. I was along to experience the ride, not control it.

As it turned out, I was the only passenger on this magical bus. There was nothing to worry about—my needs would be taken care of. I felt the promise of an unimaginable future waiting for me down the road. All I had to do was surrender. Could I do that? Could this headstrong woman, with the blood of a New Yorker still coursing through her body, hand over the reins of her life and let an unknown force decide her destiny?

Ships are safe in the harbor, but that's not what ships are for.

I thought of those words as I pondered my future. I had walked through a miraculous door into an awe-inspiring new life. I wasn't sure what was ahead of me, but one thing was certain—I was never going back. It was time to loosen the ropes that had kept this ship tethered to her past. Should my compass falter, I would sail into unknown and uncharted waters knowing I would find my course. Should I find myself shrouded in the mist, I would navigate intuitively through the fog and allow my heart to guide me. If beyond here there truly were dragons, I would spread wide my scaly wings and join their dance in the skies, knowing I, too, could breathe fire!

I had found my answer. I chose to surrender.

It was time to honor the directive that came with all I'd been given. I was ready to begin writing a new book, one that would take me in a different direction from the books I'd written for animal lovers. Somewhere in my travels, I would seek an explanation for why my personality had spontaneously changed. Why was I now doing things I would have previously considered impossible? Exactly what did happen to my brain?

My first step was to travel back in time and revisit my childhood. I knew I would find answers there explaining the choices I made in my life and how those choices had shaped the woman I'd become. If I could see the areas where I had walked, unknowingly, into the quicksand, perhaps I could help others avoid those pitfalls.

I closed my eyes, took a deep breath, and leaped off the bridge on which I stood into the swirling mist of my past. It had all started there . . . once upon a time.

Part Two

Living with Childhood Abuse in Your Past

"If the path before you is clear,
you're probably on someone else's."

—Joseph Campbell

Waiting for the Mother Ship

I'VE ALWAYS FELT A BIT disconnected from the rest of the world. I imagined myself floating in space above a giant celestial window, scanning the earth in a desperate search to locate my true family. Until I found them, I would never fit in. Somewhere along the line, I decided I must have been visiting from another planet and was accidentally left here by my fellow aliens, just like that extra-terrestrial who delighted us in the movies.

There was no question my alien family would return for me. I always envisioned it happening one night around 2:12 a.m. A blinding beam of light would come rushing through my bedroom window. A doorway would open up to the mother ship hovering outside, waiting to take me home.

"I knew you would come someday!" I'd hear myself cry with joy, as I jumped out of bed, grabbed my critters and my fringed ankle boots, ran through the doorway, and stepped onto the spaceship. There would be no sound—the ship would simply leave as quietly as it had come.

Until that day arrived, I would have to assume the body and outer trappings of an earthling and get along as best I could.

Feeling like you don't belong is one of the many common, long-term effects of childhood sexual abuse.

Other possible effects include:

- Low self-esteem
- Sleep disturbances and nightmares
- Difficulty trusting others
- Separation anxiety

- Physical ailments like gynecological, back, neck, and gastrological problems
- Drug and alcohol dependencies
- Panic attacks and flashbacks
- Feelings of sadness, fear, anger, and shame
- Feeling disconnected from the body

I lived with many of those effects, especially feeling disconnected from my body, all my life. My "little girl" abandoned me when I was very young. I never knew the joy of experiencing my world through the innocent eyes of a child. Instead, I lived in fear, always believing that something horrible was waiting for me around every corner.

The Highly Sensitive Person

THE ABUSE I ENDURED FROM my father was compounded by the fact that I am an HSP—a Highly Sensitive Person.

According to Elaine Aron, author of *The Highly Sensitive Person*,[9] this trait can be found in roughly 15–20 percent of the population and is equally divided between men and women. I remember taking the test in her book to determine if I might be an HSP. An answer of true to twelve or more of the twenty-three questions indicated high sensitivity. I answered true to twenty-two of the questions.

Dr. Aron states that stimulation is anything that wakes up the nervous system. According to an article called "Sense and Sensitivity" by Andrea Bartz,[10] published in *Psychology Today* on July 5, 2011, science and technology are now validating that highly sensitive people seem to have a nervous system that registers stimuli at a very low frequency, amplifying them internally. In general, it is upsetting if we have no control over stimulation and even more upsetting if we feel we are someone's victim.

HSPs are profoundly impacted by all that is coming at them during the day. A beautiful sunset can bring a feeling of great joy, while a taunt from the school bully, or criticism from the boss, can leave them broken and in tears. HSPs are easily overwhelmed, especially if life becomes chaotic or intense. They can sense—and internalize—the mood of others around them, so a disturbing news story about child abduction or a deadly fire can deeply upset them as they take on the emotions of the victims.

HSPs bring unique gifts to the world. They tend to fill the role of the advisor. They are the writers, philosophers, judges, teachers, and therapists. Many right-brained, creative people are highly sensitive.

Learning I was an HSP helped to answer some of the questions I'd had about myself for much of my life. It also left me heartbroken, for I now understood the depth of my inability to withstand my father's abuse and my mother's refusal to intervene.

How to Keep Justifiable Rage Hidden

ALTHOUGH I FEEL IT'S BEST to keep the details to myself, I can say that the sexual abuse I endured began when I was a young child, with certain aspects of it continuing into my early teen years. It's no wonder I was filled with rage. Once it was released, I was able to look back and see the steps I'd taken throughout my life to make certain that rage remained hidden, especially from myself.

Just like Prince Arthur's father, Uther, my father was a tyrant. He fancied himself a grand puppeteer, manipulating the people in his life with lies, threats, and physical force. He was probably six feet tall, but through the eyes of a little girl his dark presence could overshadow the tallest building. I was terrified of him.

The only happy memory I have from my childhood was going to ballet class. I started lessons when I was two and a half years old. I loved ballet because it got me out of my house a few times during the week. However, I hated recitals.

The following pages contain excerpts from *Fragments*, the piece I wrote in 1993 about how the trauma of my childhood impacted many of the decisions I made as I grew older.

From *Fragments*:

Ballet Lessons

pretty teacher
pretty music
why are all the other girls so pretty
why is this leotard so tight
I hate recitals
every year, recitals
I see two seats in the audience
one is empty
he is never there
she is in the other seat
she is very angry
I must be a very bad swan

We had a little dachshund, Schultz, who used to curl up on my bed at night. Having him near brought me comfort. One morning I woke up and discovered Schultz had been taken from me while I slept and was given to another family. My protection was gone.

After that, staying safe became my main goal in life. This meant I had to be very deliberate about my actions. I could never be carefree or exuberant or spontaneous, like little children should be. That would have meant opening myself up, which would have made me vulnerable. The only time I really opened up was when I sang, but only if I sat at the piano. The piano kept me safe.

I still have the program from my piano recital when I was eight years old. The other children played pieces called *Porky Pig*, *March of the Dwarfs* and *Sleep, Baby, Sleep*.

I played *If Ever I Would Leave You*, from *Camelot*.

I also have my report cards from third, fourth, and fifth grades. Each teacher mentioned my difficulty in speaking and how hard it was to hear my voice. It was during these years I had gone to my mother and tried to tell her what was happening to me at home. She refused to listen.

"Don't you ever talk that way about your father!" my mother said.

In the category of speaking, my fifth grade teacher graded me as GOOD (G) instead of EXCELLENT (E) and wrote these exact words on my report card: "I believe Christine is too sensitive about making a mistake when a question is asked. Therefore, she cannot even speak at all."

Under *Parent's Comments*, my mother wrote: "Would like to see the checks in the G column move to the E column."

I was not quite nine years old when I made a decision. The only way I could see my torment coming to an end was to make my father go away.

Permanently.

I stuffed a bunch of rags in the well of the window that looked into my father's basement workshop. I was in the process of setting the rags on fire when my mother found me and put a stop to my plans.

From *Fragments:*

The Dream

I dreamed about the bad one again
I dreamed that the bad thing
was happening to me
and I was scared
and I was alone

so I screamed as loud as I could
but nothing came out of my mouth
and no one heard me

I dreamed I was lost in darkness
until I saw a light
and the light became
a flame in my hand
which I set to my house
because I thought I could
burn the bad one out
and make him go away
but he wouldn't burn

and then I knew this
was no dream

As I entered my teens, I began to wonder if there was someone out there in the world who might be able to rescue me from the nightmare I was living in.

From *Fragments:*

Mist

late at night I lie in bed
and dream about a magic prince
who is out there somewhere
trying to find me
to rescue me
from the memories

he reaches out and takes my hand
I look up into his face
and there is nothing there
nothing there

I dream that this man with no face
takes me to a high hill
and tells me
if I look far into the distance
I will see the place
where I belong

so I look into the mist
and search for the place
where I belong
but there is only mist

and I know that the place
where I belong
exists only in dreams
and the person who can
take me there
exists only in my heart

When in Doubt, Run

At the age of eighteen, I made my great escape. I found a perfect apartment in Greenwich Village. The large dragon painted on the wall in the dressing room sold me on the place. My mother hired movers to spirit me out of my childhood home in Queens and deposit me in my new hideout. They showed up one Sunday morning when my father was out, and transported me, a fold-up cot, a card table, and the piano to my apartment. I thought I was safe. I thought he didn't know where I was, because Mom had put me in her phone book under a fake name. But he knew. Somehow he knew.

I wondered why Mom offered her help. At no point did she ever say she believed me. She didn't have to. We both knew the truth about the monster she was married to. This was her way of interceding on her daughter's behalf. It wasn't much, but it was all she could do.

It was a great time to live in New York City. My building was filled with people from the entertainment industry. I worked day jobs in various offices until I had put some money aside, then I'd quit and work as a singer. When the money ran out, I'd head back to the world of office administration.

It was during this time I began hearing people talk about reincarnation. Conversations on this topic ranged far and wide, and often lasted late into the night. I learned about karma, the idea that the rewards or challenges we experience in our life are a direct result of the way we lived in previous lives. When I heard we may be able to offer input in the creation of our future lives I was hooked.

I enjoyed chatting up these notions with people who were interested, and in the village that meant just about anyone you ran into. All those new concepts formed a potent cosmic stew in my teenage head. And that's when I made a gigantic mistake, one that would seal my fate with regard to the secret rage I harbored inside for my father.

I decided it must have been my actions in a previous life that landed me with an abusive father. Perhaps my current life was created for the purpose of learning how to be forgiving, a concept I may have struggled with in my past. Depositing me in a dysfunctional family with a monstrous parent would present the opportunity to extend forgiveness to my father. I could experience being merciful and compassionate. This well-intended assessment of my life may have been true, but without processing my rage—and holding the perpetrator responsible for his behavior—I set myself on a course that kept me imprisoned by my past. I continued moving forward, believing that someday I would need to forgive my father.

After living in my apartment four years, there came a day when I knew it was time to put more distance between my father and me. I began the cross country trek that would eventually lead me to Oregon. There would be three thousand miles between us. Perhaps that would make forgiving him easier.

The move to Oregon was uneventful. I missed the New York pizza and Broadway musicals, but beyond that, I settled easily into my west coast life. My third Christmas as an Oregonian was approaching. I was bringing the holiday tree up the stairs when I heard the telephone ringing in my apartment. I unlocked the door and ran to pick up the phone. My mother was sobbing on the other end. She was calling to tell me my father had died.

Christmas had come early. The man who had made my life a living hell was gone. HE WAS GONE.

I was working with a therapist at this time. When I showed up for my next visit, I told her I didn't need therapy any longer because my father had died. As far as I was concerned, I was healed.

Yeah, right.

Martha, My Forever Dog

TWO AND A HALF YEARS went by. I was driving home from work one day and saw a dog standing on the railroad tracks near my office. I parked the car and called her over. She was very thin, very bald, very flea-ridden, and very pregnant.

I took her to my vet, who thought the furry mother-to-be would be giving birth in the next few weeks. The dog needed a place to stay until I could determine if anyone was looking for her. I brought her home and introduced her to Penny, my rescue Beagle, and to Gypsy, who was a mix of all the other dog breeds. I named the new arrival Jessie. I suspected no one was searching for her. Nevertheless, I looked in all the usual *Lost Dog* places and ran an ad for a *Found Dog*. No one was interested.

Three weeks later, Jessie gave birth to six puppies in the bathroom of my 1908 Victorian home. One puppy was rather odd looking. She had black and gray fur that resembled a shag rug. Her eyes followed me wherever I went. There was something special between us. It was as if our hearts were connected by a tether woven of love and magic, but only she and I could see the rainbow-colored threads.

I named her Martha, after Paul McCartney's song *Martha My Dear*. She and Jessie became part of my family, while Jessie's other pups went on to begin their lives in five other homes. Martha may have had four legs and fur, but she would become the first true and loving parent I had ever known.

From *Fragments:*

Martha

there was a place in my heart
that was empty
the place where parents hold their
children for the first time,
embracing a miracle,
touched by grace

the place where mothers and daughters
share secrets over cups of tea
and best friends remember
a happy past

the place where lovers lie in bed
on cold winter mornings
warm and content under
piles of comforters

I knew none of these places until
one day, in the bathroom of my
old Victorian house,
a bundle of black curly fur
was born

"She's very different,"
people said
"What kind of dog is that?"
people asked
"She doesn't seem quite right,"
people commented

miracles happen
I know

Martha was a miracle
a mystic
listening to voices I would
never hear

a ribbon tying me to a
world I felt unwelcome in
until the time would come
that I knew I belonged

she was a mother, sister,
daughter, friend to me
come in the only form
I could trust

she taught me to
accept love
expect love

the empty place became smaller

I was not yet home
but when I looked down the
misty road I could see a light in
the distance

and waiting patiently
there for me
was Martha

Martha would be by my side for thirteen years. It was the loss of her in 1995 that inspired me to write my first book, *For Every Dog An Angel*.

How to Fake Forgiveness

THE YEARS PASSED. I CONTINUED on my spiritual journey, never forgetting that unfinished deed I had pushed to the back burner. I still needed to forgive my father. This is how it went in my head:

> One glorious summer night, I gathered friends and loved ones for a profound and reverent ceremony. The sky was lit with the fire of a thousand candles. Guests chanted prayers of love and celebration as I made my way into the middle of the sacred circle. I was wearing a long white dress, which billowed in the summer breeze. Tears spilled down my cheeks as I spoke the words of forgiveness. People were in awe of a woman who had been so wronged by her father, yet could release him with so much tenderness. There wasn't a dry eye in the crowd. They'd be talking about this event for years to come.

This never happened. Instead, I looked at the facts. They appeared like bullet points on a list in my brain:

- I survived his abuse.

- I fled my childhood suburban home and moved into the city to get away from him.

- I left the east coast and moved three thousand miles to get farther away from him.

- He died.

Surely, he could no longer hurt me. I decided that the *spiritual* thing to do was to simply forgive him. So that's what I did. There was no fanfare.

No chanting. No candles. No white dress. I just moved seamlessly into a peaceful, forgiving place.

There was only one problem. It was all a lie.

I forgave my father without ever expressing my rage at what he had done to me. Holding that much anger, for so long a time, took a terrible toll on me. I had found a way to survive in the world, but I would never be able to thrive. I felt like a flower that had been given just enough water to stay upright, but not enough to flourish. There is nothing noble about keeping legitimate pain and anger suppressed. You can't do anything positive for yourself, your loved ones, or the planet when you are that broken.

In looking back, I wondered if the reason I didn't know about the pent-up anger was because the part of me who felt it, the little girl, had vanished. The adult who showed up and kept me going all these years was either removed from the rage or resigned to it.

But the little girl gifted me with something precious before she left. She blessed me with a powerful imagination. It was in that fantasy world that I lived. That was where I wrote my songs about searching for a home where I truly belonged. That was where I joyfully engaged with the many beloved dogs and cats who walked by my side throughout the years. That was where I painted a meandering river up and down all the levels of my deck. And that was where my company, Lighthearted Press, was created and all the stories for animal lovers were born.

In the land of make-believe, I could nurture, grow, and preserve all the precious pieces of my life. It was in this place I could be a child and safely explore my surroundings. The fact that these explorations included eating Play-Doh behind my red toy chest is a bit disconcerting, but apparently it didn't have any long-term negative effects.

Throughout my life, I would return to my imagination as often as possible. There, I could express all the love my heart so desperately needed to share with the world. Unfortunately, the little girl did not know how to heal my heart, so I could never feel all the love that was flowing from the Universe to me in return. That would not come until many years into the future, when a prince named Arthur and a sword named Clarity made me whole again.

Part Three

The Women, the Men, and Christmas Eve

"There are only two ways to live your life.
One is as though nothing is a miracle.
The other is as though everything is a miracle."
—Albert Einstein

First Came the Women

IT BEGAN WITH STICKY NOTES.

A thought here, an idea there, quickly written on a sticky note attached to the bathroom mirror. Or the kitchen cabinet. Or the office phone. Or the garage door. Or the steering wheel of my car. Or anywhere in my house that would hold a sticky note.

FYI: sticky notes don't adhere to cats.

About two months post-*Merlin,* I gathered the sticky notes and pieced them together into something coherent. I proceeded to write the book I felt I was meant to write—the book about the miraculous healing of my childhood wounds and the unexpected gifts that came my way after watching Arthur disempower his father with the sword.

I quickly learned that writing this book would be like playing a game of hopscotch. I would be leaping over, under, and around my words as my journey continually led me to mysterious and unexpected places.

One day I mentioned my new book to someone who had called to place an order. I began doing this from time to time, always being cautious about whom I shared the story with and how many details I offered. One by one, women began offering me their stories in return.

They came to me in whispered phone calls, tentatively written emails, and social media messages. Women who were familiar with my books for animal lovers were surprised to learn that I, too, had endured childhood abuse. It was as if an author who wrote whimsical books, where dogs fly through starry skies and cats soar in whipped cream clouds, couldn't possibly have navigated her way through a nightmare of a childhood. The knowledge that my lighthearted books didn't reflect a lighthearted past seemed to reach out to women.

Their stories touched me deeply. Their courage touched me even more. One woman told me how her younger brother and sister, at the ages of six and eight respectively, were sexually abused by their mother's former boyfriend. It was a note scribbled in crayon and left on the edge of the bathtub that alerted the family to the situation.

Another woman called to tell me that her daughter had been assaulted by a school custodian when the girl was young. The daughter later entered an abusive marriage, and her mother was extremely worried for the safety of her daughter and grandsons.

A third woman I spoke with told me she'd had a sexually abusive step-father, who made certain she knew every day how worthless she was. At the age of sixteen, she was raped by five men and kept the resulting pregnancy to herself for eight months. She was hidden away at a hospital and left on her own to deliver her daughter. She returned to school as if nothing had happened.

The more people I told about my book, the more I began noticing an unnerving pattern. Just about everyone had their own story to share.

I hadn't planned on writing much about my own journey with abuse. I thought the quantum change that freed me from the rage needed to be mentioned, but not necessarily explored. I was wrong. It was a phone call from a client that resulted in my path taking yet another turn.

She had called to place a gift order for one of my books. We got to chatting, and I mentioned I was working on a new book that wouldn't be about animals. I shared just a few sentences—I had gone through a miraculous experience that freed me from years of rage I'd carried due to childhood abuse. I said I'd let her know when the book became available.

She called back later that evening, about eight o'clock, her time. Her abuse was not from her childhood—it was from her first marriage. She has been re-married for thirty-five years, but felt more comfortable talking with me after her husband had gone to bed. She knew she couldn't go to sleep without following her heart and calling to tell me I had her support in writing this book.

I was beginning to hear this often. I wasn't a therapist or a trained professional in the area of abuse. That didn't seem to matter. Just letting other women know I had walked a difficult path and had made my way to the other side seemed to offer a beacon of hope. If I could find my way through the darkness, perhaps they could, too.

Then Came the Men

WHEN I BEGAN WORKING ON this book I thought I'd be writing primarily for, about, and because of women. Once again, I was mistaken. It seemed my book was meant to be touched by the wisdom, energy, generosity, and compassion of many gentle men who unexpectedly found their way to my story.

On a cloudless, late-summer day in 2012, I headed out on a long drive down the magnificent Columbia River. I had just purchased the *Secrets of Manifesting*[11] CD set by Dr. Wayne Dyer, and it seemed like the perfect time to begin listening to them. I was engrossed in his words when he suddenly mentioned something about quantum moments, a profound awakening of spirit that many people have reported experiencing. The moment is vivid, unexpected, benevolent, and lasting.

What? What had he said?

I replayed those last few sentences and started to shake. He was describing exactly what had happened to me after I watched that episode of *Merlin*! When I got home, I went online and read more about Dr. Dyer's comments on the subject. He mentioned a book called *Quantum Change: When Epiphanies and Sudden Insights Transform Ordinary Lives*,[12] by psychologists William R. Miller and Janet C'de Baca.

I bought the book and began reading it immediately. It was filled with the first-hand stories of people whose lives had been transformed by these unexpected moments. Everything I had experienced was described in perfect detail within its pages.

I was deeply moved by this thoughtful book. It provided insights and answers to questions still forming in my mind. The authors were respectful of the contributors and their stories. I read an interview Dr. Miller gave in 2008, in which he said he thought his work on quantum change was the most important piece he had done in thirty-five years. It was obvious he was touched by the people who had opened their hearts and shared their miraculous moments, many of whom had kept these stories to themselves for years.

In their closing comment, the authors said they could not fully account for why these quantum changes occur. They offered these words:

"It comes even to those not seeking it, not even aware of a need or possibility for such deep renewal. It is as though life delights in taking us by surprise, tapping us on the shoulder and reminding us now and again of how very little we really know of all that is possible."[13]

Quantum Change became a treasured friend as I continued along on my journey. It would be several months before I contacted Dr. Miller and asked if I might be able to speak with him about my experience. He graciously said yes.

Reading *Quantum Change* gave me momentum. I was making good progress on the book, but I needed to bounce my ideas off others and get some feedback.

It was a Monday night, and I was working late in my office. I'd been without phone service for three days and had become a bit snarky about it. The telephone repair person was coming the following morning. I decided to wrap up the writing for the day and pick it back up on Tuesday.

I was at the computer the next day when the doorbell rang. In came Jeff, the repairman, who quickly determined there was a glitch with the wiring in my office. He parked himself a few feet away from me to fix the problem.

While Jeff worked on the wiring, I sat at my computer, staring at the manuscript. For a moment it looked like it had been written in hieroglyphics. What was I trying to say? I needed a new perspective—and I needed it quickly.

For reasons I can't explain, I looked over at Jeff and asked if he had ever watched a television show called *Merlin*. Unfortunately, he was not familiar with the show. I turned back to the monitor. About thirty seconds later he asked me why I had posed that question. I said I was writing a book about something miraculous that had happened several months earlier when I was watching a specific episode of the show.

A few more moments went by, and then he asked for details. I gave him a brief explanation of what I'd experienced, how my life had been transformed, and how my brain had been rewired in that one incredible moment.

I assumed he would go back to his work. Instead, he responded in a language I can only call *brainspeak*. He began telling me about how the different parts of the brain work. My eyes opened very wide. *How did he know this?*

I started to tell him what I had learned in the book *Quantum Change* by Dr. William Miller.

"Bill Miller?" he asked.

"You know his work?" I was speechless.

Jeff told me that until recently he had been studying to become a therapist. Dr. Miller's books on motivational interviewing were among those used by students in that field. I ran to grab my copy of *Quantum Change* and showed him all my paper-clipped and yellow-highlighted pages. He put down the wires he was trimming. We spent the next hour talking about the brain.

I will be forever grateful it was Jeff who showed up at my home that day. Of course, it was meant to be Jeff. He may have been a telephone repairman by trade, but to me, he will always be an angel in a tool belt.

Many other men joined me on my journey.

There was the salesman I met in the electronics store. We started talking about our work, and I told him about the book I was writing. He looked me in the eye and said that he, too, had endured sexual abuse in his past. He talked about how he had dealt with the trauma. Many women had told me their stories, but this was the first man to share his ordeal with me.

There was another friend who talked about the burden of being a man in this day and age. His property is adjacent to a walking path that goes through a wooded area. He said he understands how women might be afraid of meeting a man on that path. If he sees a woman coming in his direction, he consciously assumes a non-threatening body posture and tries to be as easy-going as possible. He is one of the kindest men I've ever met. The thought of him being perceived as menacing is laughable. Yet, if I didn't know him and I was coming down that path, I might be concerned, too.

There was Tom, a man I met at the mall. I can't recall why we began talking about my book, but suddenly we connected on a metaphysical level that was astonishing. I told him I'd originally thought my book would be about and for women, but I was unexpectedly delighted that so many kind and open-hearted men had come to join me on my adventure. Tom told me, "An integration of the two energies, contained in each of us, can heal the tear." He also shared several stories and quotes that touched me deeply, including this one:

"You cannot heal the divine feminine without causing a simultaneous and equal healing of the divine masculine. And vice versa. When these energies get untangled and emerge from shadow, they support each other."—Howard Jacobson

There was Jason, who generously offered his time to help me understand the concept of being one with the sword. He was infinitely more graceful than I and had the patience of a saint. I'll always be grateful our paths crossed.

And there was Michael, my former husband, whose many years of leading men's groups made him the perfect gentle warrior to offer me guidance. He knew me well, for we were together twenty years. The sword didn't come back to my hand until Michael and I had parted, but when it came to understanding shields and being courageous, he was there to provide the male perspective.

The Return of Merlin

MY FAVORITE LINE IN THE 1967 movie, *Camelot,* occurs when King Arthur meets Lancelot for the first time. Arthur remembers Merlin once telling him that Lancelot would be the greatest knight to sit at his table, but that was long before Arthur had ever thought of creating the round table. In that moment, Arthur realizes he has stumbled onto his future.

As a writer (and a reader) I am very fortunate to live in the city that is home to Powell's, the largest independent new and used bookstore in the world. It's a thrill to walk through this store. The smell of the books is intoxicating.

I always have a running list of titles I want to purchase. Given the book I was writing, it seemed like the perfect time to add *The Once and Future King, The Book of Merlin,* and *Le Morte d'Arthur* to my library. Then I added one more book to my list. In searching online for a quotation, I saw a reference to the book *The Return of Merlin,*[14] by Deepak Chopra. I have other books by the author, but this one was new to me. It was his first novel, published in 1995, and it sounded intriguing. With my list in hand, I headed downtown to spend several enchanting hours in Powell's.

That night I picked up *The Return of Merlin,* curled up in front of the fire, and fell effortlessly into the pages of the book. I was captivated by the story and willingly surrendered to the magic of the author's words. It was tempting to stay up all night with the book, but I decided to read just a few pages at a time so I could be with the story for as long as possible.

By this time, I was many months into the writing of my own book. *The Return of Merlin* proved to be the perfect companion as I continued down my path. Deepak Chopra had created a mesmerizing world. The characters were so real I longed to stand in their presence and lay before them the puzzle pieces of my life. I was certain they could help me understand why I had been miraculously transformed by Prince Arthur and why my journey had been touched by Camelot ever since I was a little girl. The characters in Dr. Chopra's book became friends, and I knew it would be difficult to say goodbye to them.

The day came when I was down to the last ten pages. *The Return of Merlin* balanced on the top of a stack of books on the end table in the living room. Before I sat down to finish the story, I ran upstairs to grab one other title off the bookshelf.

I know my books well. They're grouped by categories on specific shelves. I scanned the shelf at eye level. I thought I saw something, so I went back and scanned that shelf again. My heart stopped. There, right in front of me, was *The Return of Merlin*. It was a hard-covered first edition of the book . . . and it was autographed by Deepak Chopra. Inside, was a 1995 flyer from Powell's Books welcoming Deepak Chopra in his presentation of his first work of fiction.

I had no idea how that book came to be on my shelf. I'd never heard of the book. I had no memory of ever attending a book-signing by this brilliant man. I only have a few books that are signed by the author, and I certainly would have remembered bringing home a book that was autographed by an author I admire so much.

I held the book in my hand and tried to imagine how it possibly could have found its way to my bookshelf without my knowing it. If I attended that book signing, the memory of it was completely gone from my mind.

I closed my eyes and turned the book over and over, my fingers caressing the dust jacket. I felt the words coming out of the paper, imprinting themselves on my skin. A gentle wind began to move softly in the room. It came through a magical forest, hidden somewhere in time, and the scent of the trees surrounded me. The wind touched the story I held in my hands, working its way into the pages. The book contained the answer I needed and was eager to reveal itself to me.

As quickly as it had begun, the wind came to a stop. The room was quiet. And then I heard something. It was a voice from long ago. It had come to this very room in 1995, on the day *The Return of Merlin* was mysteriously added to my bookshelf.

You don't know about this book yet, Chris. I heard the voice with perfect clarity. *But eighteen years from now you will find it exactly when you are meant to find it. In that moment, you will understand something very important. It will help to explain your journey.*

And, suddenly, I did understand. I knew it didn't matter how the book had come to be in my possession. There was only one thing that did matter.

I had stumbled onto my future.

"Life is full of mystery and magic and the miraculous and the wondrous. And when we have flashes of wonder, that's when we experience the world of the wizard."—Deepak Chopra

Becoming Fearless

"You've changed," my friends told me.

I began to hear this often. I was no longer the beaten-down woman who had somehow managed to stagger through her life. I stood taller, with my head held high. My new-found confidence was evident, especially to the family and friends who knew me before.

I had always tried to attract the people, energy, and synchronistic events that would help me carry out my destiny, never realizing the anger I held inside was a barrier that would keep this from occurring. With the rage released, I was suddenly in the flow. Whatever I needed to fulfill my life's purpose could now effortlessly make its way to me. Anything was possible. My days of living in the shadows were over. An unfamiliar feeling was surfacing.

I was becoming fearless.

The challenges and opportunities that previously sent me running now beckoned me. I knew that people would never speak about me as I had often spoken of my mother.

"She had so much potential," I used to say about Mom.

In the book, *The Top Five Regrets of the Dying* by Bronnie Ware,[15] the author states the most common regret of those at the end of their lives is wishing they'd had the courage to live a life true to themselves, not the life others had expected of them.

I prefer to go out this way: "Life should not be a journey to the grave with the intention of arriving safely in a pretty and well preserved body, but rather to skid in broadside in a cloud of smoke, thoroughly used up, totally worn out, and loudly proclaiming "Wow! What a ride!"—Hunter S. Thompson

Run Toward the Roar

THIS TEACHING STORY TAKES PLACE on the African savannas. As herds move across the plains, lions wait in the tall grasses, eager for a chance to prey upon the unsuspecting animals. The oldest and weakest of the lions have often lost all their teeth and are no longer capable hunters.

They can, however, roar. So they take their place in the tall grass, across from the younger lions who are the skilled hunters.

As the herds make their way into the area between the old lions and the young ones, the old lions let out a thunderous roar. This sends the terrified herds running in the opposite direction, directly into the pack of young lions waiting to claim their dinner.

When faced with danger, run toward the roar.

"In times of trouble or tragedy, a person either steps into life more fully or else slips into a diminished life characterized by fear and anxiety."
—Michael Meade

Christmas Eve: The Night the Magic Ended

I HAD BECOME FEARLESS. I was now a woman who could attract all that she needed to manifest her life's true purpose. Little did I know it was all about to come crashing down around me.

It began on December 11, 2012. I was looking forward to meeting a friend for lunch. A stop at the mall was also on my agenda. Should I go before or after lunch? I decided to go before, so after running my errand, I headed to the restaurant.

I was home by three o'clock. About an hour or so later, my neighbor, Paula, called and told me to turn on the TV—there was a shooter at the mall. My mall. The mall a mile from my home. The mall I'd been in that morning. The mall I would have been in when the shooter was there, had I chosen to go after my lunch date.

The horrific scene was plastered all over the local and national news. Helicopters began arriving immediately. The sky above my home filled with the sound of non-stop chopping as their blades beat the air. When the gunfire ended, the heartbreaking news came that two people had been killed and a teenage girl had been badly wounded. The shooter took his life.

Something happened to me that night. The relentless noise of the helicopters made me feel like I was trapped in a war zone. Unable to find a foxhole, I crouched down low in my bedroom and heard myself gasping for air. After several hours, I took an over-the-counter sleeping pill, stuffed in a pair of ear plugs, put a pillow over my head, and eventually fell asleep. The helicopters were still circling in the morning.

Three days later, in what would become the second deadliest school shooting in U.S. history, a gunman shot and killed twenty children and six adult staff members at an elementary school in Connecticut. He killed his mother before coming to the school and ended his rampage by killing himself. Our nation mourned, and the world mourned with us. Our hearts broke for all the families whose lives had been shattered that day.

The second shooting sent me spiraling into a deep, dark chasm. The grief from these two events closed in around me. I was terrified—for myself and for every human being on the planet. I couldn't think about Christmas or decorating a tree. My folk-art Nativity display sat in its box. The dog I had created for the display, the one that went with my book *Old Dog and the Christmas Wish*, would not watch over the Child this year.

I found it difficult to continue with the book. With each passing day, I doubted, more and more, my ability to finish the book. I had experienced a miracle—a quantum change—that altered me on so many levels I was no longer the same person. I had been told I was meant to share the story, but suddenly I felt lost. The miraculous doorway connecting me to a television show in a faraway land was closing. The magical sword that had finally found its way to my hand was slipping back into the mist.

So many extraordinary gifts had been given to me this year, yet I could not find a light out of my darkness. It was clear the Universe had made a colossal mistake. Maybe the quantum change was meant to go to the man down the road or to the woman in the next county. It had surely never been intended for me. I looked up to the heavens and cried, "You should have given this miracle to a worthy person!"

There was one thought I had been keeping at bay, a final thought that would sink me so far into the abyss I wasn't sure I'd be able to find my way out. It would culminate on Christmas Eve, the same day *Merlin* was ending its five-year run on television. (Even though it wouldn't be available in the States until January 2013, I'd been following the show throughout the fall online, as it aired overseas.)

On December 24th, at four o'clock in the afternoon, I sat down at my computer and watched the final episode of the show that had transformed my life. It was perfection . . . and it was gut-wrenching. As the word *Merlin* flashed across the screen for the last time, the thought I had been dreading for two weeks finally found its way to my heart—the mystical experience that had touched my life, the unexpected journey that began with *Merlin* would now end with *Merlin*, as the show, itself, drew to a close. I was not deserving of the gifts I'd been given. I would leave the book unfinished. It was time to lay down my sword.

I went into my kitchen, sat in darkness at the table, and put my head in my hands. I heard the clock in my office ticking as the minutes went by. Something made me look up. I saw three boxes sitting on the kitchen counter—gifts from friends and family I'd been saving to open on Christmas Day.

"Oh, what the hell."

I walked over and picked up the first box. It was from my dear friend, Judy, who lives in Florida. Judy is twenty-two years my senior—old enough to feel like a mother to me, yet so young in spirit I never think about the difference in our ages. She is a passionate and lifelong dog and cat lover, whose home is always open to those critters needing a little extra love or attention. She has a special place in her heart for English bulldogs and works closely with their local rescue group. Judy also loves the Miami Dolphins, NASCAR, opera, and politics.

I knew that my journey with the sword wasn't exactly her cup of tea. "Well, Chris," she told me early on, "I don't know about this sword thing, but I love you and I'll read your book." Although we spoke and emailed all the time, I kept much of my adventures with the blade to myself.

Judy's box was marked *fragile*. There was another box inside, with something wrapped in many layers of paper. I carefully peeled the paper away, watching as the gift began to reveal itself. When the last of the paper fell to the floor, I was left holding something so exquisite I thought my heart would take wing and fly around the room.

There, in my hands, was a glass dragon sword. It was not quite nine inches long. The cross-guard was in the shape of a dragon. Its head of gold, with a single red eye, sat in the middle, and its red wings stretched to either side. Golden dragon scales ran down the blade.

I dropped to my knees, cradling the glass gift in my arms, and fell into choking sobs. Judy's magical sword was pointing the way back to the journey I thought had come to an end. I picked up the phone and dialed Judy's number. I tried, through my tears, to tell her what she had done for me. She listened patiently, surprised at all the suffering I had kept to myself.

"Chris," she said, "I know you like blues and greens, but this sword only came in red and gold."

"It's perfect, Judy," I told her. "Those are the colors of Camelot!"

The second gift came from my California friend, Kathleen. Her home is filled with the many dogs and cats who have luckily found their way to her. Kathleen is also a passionate horsewoman, whose stories about their mystical nature led me to include two magical horses in my book, *Forever Paws*.

You need only spend a few moments with Kathleen to know she must be a heavenly being who has chosen to live among us mortals for a time. I felt joy emanating from the package she sent because that's how it is with Kathleen—she wraps everything with love. When I opened her box, I found something as captivating as the woman who had sent it. There, floating in a ball of glass, sat a dragon resting atop a medieval castle. Kathleen had gifted me with a dragon snow globe.

The little girl inside jumped up and down with delight. A dragon! One of the reasons I enjoyed *Merlin* so much was the presence of the great dragon in the story. For the second time that night, I felt myself being called back into the mystery. Kathleen's gift beckoned to my inner child—the one who had only recently returned to my heart. "Do you want to come out and play?" the dragon whispered. "Oh, yes!" I cried.

One package remained. It had been sent by my younger brother, Jim, who lives in Michigan with his family. I deeply and genuinely love my brother. I still remember when he was born and I was only allowed to hold him cradled in a pillow.

My sense of humor is a lot like Jim's, which means we can pretty much make a joke about anything. In the big scheme of things, though, our personalities are very different. I am the dreamer, with a path that zigzags across the stars. Jim navigates by a different compass, one I don't always understand but I do respect. Many a time, I have called him for advice, grateful for the wisdom he has gathered by following that compass.

I was eager to share the wild ride I'd been on ever since I saw that twenty-first episode of *Merlin*. Who could better understand what it was like to be freed from my haunted childhood than the brother who lived in the same household? I would mention a snippet here and there, always saying I'd give him more details when we had a chance to speak further.

As the months went by, I began to sense that revisiting the past might be uncomfortable for Jim. I desperately wanted to pass along the miraculous gifts I'd received, but I had to accept that this was my journey, not his. The world of swords, quantum changes, and brain chemistry was probably not meant to intersect with Jim's world. He needed to follow his own path.

My brother's gift came in a flat box. Perhaps a scarf or something for the cats? I opened the package and let out a gasp. How could he possibly have known I needed these? For that matter, how could he have even known what these were?

My brother sent me something every person who carries a sword needs— leather gauntlet gloves. I had been meaning to buy a pair, because the multiple cords I wrapped around Clarity's hilt made it tricky to hold her without some type of protection. The tears fell as I pulled on the gloves and walked over to my desk. "Well, my dear," I said, picking up the sword that had found its way to my hand. "I guess our journey isn't over after all."

I sat down at the kitchen table, marveling at the events that had transpired. Just as the road I'd been traveling gave way under my feet, three gifts came that undeniably showed me the way back to my path. My journey was not over—it was just beginning! I was filled with a profound sense of wonder. Judy, Kathleen, and Jim were as different from each other as three people could be. They had never met and probably never would. The only thing they had in common was their love for me. With that love guiding the way, they had set a plan in motion that brought my hurting heart exactly what it needed for healing at the moment I needed it most.

On Christmas day, I called Kathleen and Jim and shared the story of what happened the night before. How do you appropriately express your gratitude to someone for collaborating on a Christmas Eve miracle?

My next call was to my ex-husband, Michael. I told him everything that had happened to me after the shooting at the mall. "You need a shield," Michael said. I told him I hoped to get one someday, but I didn't have one yet.

"Not an actual shield, Chris." Then he proceeded to tell me about a piece he does with the men's group he leads. The symbolic shield is used to help men determine what can safely be let through and what needs to be deflected. That image made everything clear to me. I'd been doing it all wrong! I had allowed all the sorrow and suffering in the world to come rushing through my shield, overwhelming me to the point of being incapacitated. What was more astonishing, I had deflected the friends and family who would have been able to support me in my time of despair, if only I had asked for their help.

I was beginning to understand why I was so susceptible to the sadness that had disabled me. When I began my magical odyssey, I was told I needed to trust the mystery and surrender to the journey. I was able to do that because I felt I was being guided by a loving and benevolent Universe. Surrendering had made me vulnerable, which wasn't a problem until the first shooting occurred in my own front yard. From that point on, I was defenseless. I had gone into the same mode I used as a child to survive my father. I blocked everyone out and proceeded as if I were on my own.

Michael was right—I needed to learn how to use a shield. I thanked him for being one of my teachers during this extraordinary Christmas. I looked once again to the heavens, only this time I didn't cry out my unworthiness for the gifts that had been bestowed upon me. Instead, I offered prayers of gratitude for the loved ones who had come to guide me out of the darkness.

It was hard to comprehend all that had happened to me on one magical Christmas Eve. Suddenly, I was as light as a feather—just like Ebenezer Scrooge on Christmas morning!

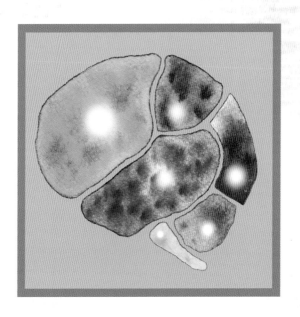

Part Four

The Magical Brain

"You have brains in your head.
You have feet in your shoes.
You can steer yourself
any direction you choose."
—Dr. Seuss (Oh, the Places You'll Go!)[16]

Can We Consciously Change Our Brain?

SO MUCH HAD CHANGED SINCE I watched *Merlin*. My perception of who I was had completely shifted. I only ate when I was hungry. I was no longer comfortable wearing the shapeless clothes in my closet. I now saw myself as a woman who carried a sword.

All of these changes were perplexing, but perhaps most astounding was twenty-five years of debilitating spinal pain coming to a screeching halt. It was time to start asking questions. How could this have happened? For that matter, how could any of these things have happened? I hadn't done anything purposefully to create them. I felt alive. I'd been given the courage to pursue whatever called to my heart. Anything—absolutely anything—was possible. I was eager to share this feeling of ecstasy with every person on the planet. "Here, drink this!" I wanted to say as I put a magic elixir in their hand. "I want you to feel as joyful and passionate about your life as I do!"

One day, I sat down at the computer and typed these words into the search engine: Can we consciously change our brain? I had no idea how extraordinary a turn my journey was about to take.

So, can we consciously change our brain? Let's start with the piano.

Volunteers with no piano experience participated in an experiment at Harvard Medical School. They were divided into groups. One group of volunteers practiced a piano exercise, on a piano, for two hours a day. After five days, tests showed that the part of the brain associated with learning this exercise had changed. New connections had been made.

A second group of volunteers were asked to think about playing the piano exercise. Their hands never touched a keyboard. They played the music in their heads and imagined moving their fingers over the keys.

When this group was tested, their brains experienced the same changes as the group that had physically played the piano. The brain couldn't tell the difference between playing the piano with one's fingers and playing the piano in one's mind.

How could this be?

Neuroplasticity

THE BRAIN IS MADE UP of approximately 100 billion nerve cells, called neurons. Until recently, scientists believed the brain was hardwired with a fixed number of neurological connections, incapable of changing once we passed childhood. But new research and advances in technology tell us the brain never stops changing. It continues to grow throughout our lifetime. And, yes, we can consciously change the connections in the brain.

The ability of our brain to form new neural connections in response to learning, changes in behavior and environment, and changes resulting from bodily injury and disease is called neuroplasticity.

The brain responds to our thoughts and experiences. However, it can't tell the difference between what is happening in the external world and what is happening in our imagination. This explains the new connections created in the brains of the volunteers who never touched a piano but only practiced the music in their mind.

Every thought signals the brain to release a chemical into the bloodstream, matching an emotion to the thought. If thoughts are uplifting and positive, the brain releases chemicals that make the person feel uplifted and positive. If thoughts are angry or fearful, the brain releases chemicals that cause angry or fearful feelings.

Since our thoughts tell the brain how we want to feel, it behooves us to be conscious of what we are thinking throughout the day. Author and motivational speaker, Mike Dooley, puts it this way: "Thoughts are things— choose the good ones!"

Where Did My Pain Go?

IF YOU HAVE EVER LIVED with constant pain, you know how deeply it impacts your life. Your sleep is impaired, which means your waking hours suffer from lack of rest. Decision-making is compromised. Exhaustion makes it challenging to care about what you eat or how much exercise you get. You look in the mirror and wonder who is that person? At some point, you resign yourself to doing only what must be done to keep your life going. Everything else falls to the side.

A large portion of my adult life fell within those parameters. The thought that my pain could end—completely and instantaneously—never crossed my mind. I wouldn't have believed it possible. And yet, that is exactly what happened the moment my rage was lifted from me.

So, what caused twenty-five years of spinal pain to come to an end after watching Merlin? The question wouldn't go away.

Midway through my year-long odyssey, I bought the book *Train Your Mind, Change Your Brain*[17] by Sharon Begley. Ms. Begley is currently the senior health and science correspondent at Reuters, reporting on neuroscience, genetics, cognitive science, and other research. At the time she wrote her book, she was the science editor and science columnist at Newsweek.

The cover of *Train Your Mind, Change Your Brain* includes the words *A Groundbreaking Collaboration between Neuroscience and Buddhism*. The foreword of the book is written by The Dalai Lama. The back of the book mentions the brain's ability to heal and renew itself after trauma. I contacted Ms. Begley and asked if she could shed any light on what might have happened to my spinal pain. She gave me permission to share her thoughts, clarifying that she is a journalist, not a scientist or doctor.

Ms. Begley hypothesized about "the sudden release of brain opiates flooding the pain centers or the somatosensory cortex in such a way as to vanquish the pain, or signals from the cortex (where the memories of the abuse were processed) surging out to the insula (which contains a representation of the body) so as to eliminate the pain."

Was it possible the overwhelming joy I experienced (once my rage was gone) led to the release of potent, pain-killing chemicals into my bloodstream? And did these chemicals find their way to the pain center in my brain and instantly end my suffering?

I spoke with a marriage and family therapist who uses the latest scientific findings about the brain in her work. I asked her if releasing my rage led me to instantly rewrite my life story. Did I go from being a tormented victim of sexual abuse to an empowered woman who carries a sword and knows that we can overcome past trauma? Did that immediate transformation cause an overload of joy-inducing chemicals to flood and rewire my brain? She told me yes—that was most likely what happened.

It's a Wonderful Life

ARE YOU READY TO CREATE a new reality for yourself? Excellent—there's no time like the present! Before you begin, however, you might want to take a quick peek at who you're bringing to the starting line. If you're looking to change your life, you can't show up dragging the same old hopeless personality with its limiting beliefs and dismal outlook. You're going to have to bring someone new—someone with an infectious spirit and positive attitude—to the table.

We already know the brain can't tell the difference between what is imagined and what is actually happening. With that in mind, here are a few strategies that keep me aligned with the magnificent life I was given:

- Begin by being aware of your thoughts.

- Be clear about the new reality you desire. See all the details.

- Hold the vision firmly in your mind. Do this throughout your day.

- Know that your brain is structurally changing to accommodate your desire, for it believes the event has already happened.

- The brain alters itself every time it learns something new. Encourage your brain to make new connections by changing your habits. If you always brush your teeth with the right hand, switch to the left hand. If you drive the same route to work every day, look for a different path requiring your attention.

- Be aware of any thoughts or emotions that keep you connected to your past. With time, you will be able to keep them effortlessly out of your life. (Several "sentries"—including dogs, cats, and dragons—have volunteered to help me with this task!)

- Every morning, before you get out of bed, ask what would be the very best expression of yourself to bring to the world that day. (True confession: sometimes I just ask what would be the most fun I could have today!)

- Remember, you are letting go of the old self and reinventing a new you. There are no limitations to who you can be.

- Dream BIG!

Part Five

The Seven Gifts

"There is no such thing as a problem without
a gift for you in its hands. You seek problems
because you need their gifts."
—Richard Bach (Illusions)[18]

Honor Where You Are

IT WAS ALL ABOUT THE fringed ankle boots.

A few months had passed since my quantum change. I was used to feeling on top of the world. My energy was high and my path was clear. While walking through a store in the mall, something caught my eye— ankle boots with fringe down the side, two of my favorite things in life. The boots were calling to me. "No!" I yelled back. "I don't need another pair of ankle boots, fringed or not."

I headed to my car, proud that I had put those boots in their place and that place was not in my closet.

So why was I feeling sad?

When I got home, I threw myself on the bed and tried to understand what was happening to me. I knew my brain was dumping chemicals into my bloodstream that mirrored my thoughts, which would keep me mired in the sadness. I needed to break the thought process immediately.

I dragged myself off the bed and stood in front of the mirror. Yikes! Where had these come from? I was wearing some of the tent-like clothing I saved as mementoes from my past. I wasn't aware I had put these on, but my body certainly was . . . and it wasn't happy.

This isn't who you are anymore. The voice came from somewhere inside me. *This isn't where you are, either.*

Hello? Exactly who is speaking?

You need to honor where you are.

Honor where I am? Where, exactly, was I?

Back in your body—that's where! You are a fully integrated person!

At the beginning of my incredible journey, I experienced something I didn't think would ever happen. I had stood in my closet of shame and felt the trauma I'd put my body through by spending a lifetime dressing in shapeless, oversized clothes. I had looked, with wide-eyed wonder, at the reflection smiling back at me. I saw in her the young girl who fled in fear, the lost teenager who continually thought of running away, and the woman who had spent a lifetime living in her imagination. They were all one now, and in coming back together, they—and I—had found peace.

I was in awe of this woman. She was joyful and optimistic and vulnerable. And that's when the unimaginable happened. I fell helplessly and hopelessly in love with her. Out had gone most of those baggy garments. I promised myself I would no longer be incognito.

But I had not kept that promise. The clothing I saw as I stood in front of the mirror said otherwise. I ripped off the offensive garments and replaced them with my skinny jeans and body-hugging t-shirt. The outfit looked great. All it needed was a pair of . . . fringed ankle boots.

An hour later, I was back home sporting my new footwear. I finally got the message. My quantum change had given me the opportunity to experience life as a complete being—heart, soul, and body. The heart and soul parts always came naturally, but being connected to my body was new. The Universe had given me a priceless gift. To go back to dressing as a broken, lost girl was dishonoring the gift.

Honor where you are. The fringed ankle boots brought this lesson home for me. What will it be for you?

Seek Help When You Need It

ASKING FOR HELP—IT WAS A foreign concept to me. I told my mother about the abuse my father was subjecting me to, and she refused to listen. I learned at an early age that if I was suffering, no one would offer me a shoulder to lean on. I was on my own.

Had I been raised to believe my feelings mattered, I would have confided in someone about the fear I felt after the shooting at my mall. But I couldn't bring myself to share my terror with anyone. I wasn't afraid of appearing weak if I said I was struggling. I simply believed I was so worthless no one would care if I was suffering. If I asked for help, and everyone turned away from me, I would once again be reminded of my insignificance.

When I opened the holiday gifts from afar, I was carried out of my sorrow by the love that filled each package. I felt the presence of these three special people, who wanted me to know I was not alone that Christmas Eve. I could sit in peace within their circle. They would hold up a shield for me. They would make a place for my grief. They would witness my tears.

The Universe had sent me my own three wise men, only in this case it was two wise women and my very wise brother. They found a way to let me know that if I was hurting, it mattered to them. I mattered to them.

Seek help when you need it and help will always come.

I finally understood those words. O, Holy Night, indeed.

Practice Giveaway

The first time I heard the word *giveaway* was in 1995, two years before I wrote my book *For Every Dog An Angel*. I was looking to leave the corporate world and find a way of making a living that would celebrate my love for animals. With my dog, Martha, by my side, I felt certain I would find my soul work.

I met with my friend, Misa Hopkins, a healer of Native American descent, who I hoped could offer guidance for my journey.

"What will be your giveaway?" Misa asked me.

I wasn't sure what she was talking about, so she explained that when you are inviting something new into your life, you often need to make space for it. I came to understand this might mean giving up something tangible, or it might mean letting go of a belief or philosophy that could prevent you from living your dream.

In true "Chris" fashion, I told her exactly what my giveaway would be—Brussels sprouts. You have to understand how much I don't care for Brussels sprouts to appreciate how pitiful that answer was. Here I was, seeking to create something magnificent in my life, and in exchange, I was willing to give up a vegetable I detested. I was not off to an impressive start.

A few weeks later, I came home and found Martha standing motionless in the yard. She had gone into a catatonic state. Veterinary experts were called in to determine what was going on in Martha's brain. I was confident we would find the answers and my beautiful girl would be restored to health. Instead, I lost Martha fifteen days after she became ill.

The Universe had decided for me. Martha was to be my giveaway.

Broken-hearted over my loss, I met with a woman who had been instrumental in helping me envision my new life's work. "Elaine, I have fallen off my path," I told her. "No, you haven't," she said. "It just looks different than you thought it would."

Martha left me in October 1995. It was the devastating loss of her that led me to write *For Every Dog An Angel*, a book that celebrates the timeless connection between people and their forever dogs. A few weeks after her passing, I saw an angel in the sky holding Martha in her arms. Two years later, that vision would become the cover of *For Every Dog An Angel*.

Purging all the rage I held inside from my traumatic childhood had been the biggest giveaway of my life. As it had been with Martha, I didn't make this giveaway consciously. Once again, the Universe decided for me.

I'm learning to bring more awareness to this area. If my life feels off balance, I ask myself if there is something in me that no longer fits and needs to be set free. With Clarity's help, I envision myself cutting away what is no longer needed and attaching it to a balloon filled with a golden light. I open my hand and let the balloon go, watching as the golden glow disappears into the sky. I am left with gratitude for all that remains, for that is what is important to me.

Surrender to Your Journey

DEFINITION OF SURRENDER: TO GIVE in, abandon, let go, yield, or relinquish.

One of the sweetest gifts of my life-changing odyssey was learning how—and when—to surrender. It was a term that had been low on my vocabulary list. After all, if you go through life believing you are on your own, then you also must be the one who keeps all the spinning plates perfectly balanced in the air. Giving in isn't an option. If you yield, the plates will come crashing down, your world will collapse, and everything you hold dear will be destroyed.

This belief made me self-sufficient, which wasn't necessarily a bad thing, until I realized it reinforced the message in my head that no one would come to my aid if I needed it.

When I began my journey, I knew I would have to surrender to it. Completely. It was the price of admission if I wanted to fully experience all that had been given to me. I would have to step blindly into the mystery, accepting the fact that I had no idea what might happen. It would mean removing the name tag that said *Chris Davis—managing my world every step of the way, on my own, until the end of time.* I did this willingly, because somehow I knew surrendering to this miracle would not diminish or endanger me. Instead, it would expand and empower me.

It became clear that I would have to abandon my schedule for completing the manuscript, because the book had its own timetable. My road took many twists and turns, often bringing something unexpected that fit perfectly into the book, but would require additional weeks or months to research and write.

For the first time in my career as an author, I put my writing in front of others who agreed to read it and offer feedback. This act represented yet another surrender—letting go of the belief that I was the only one who could possibly know the best way to tell my story. I honor the integrity and courage of all the readers who lovingly, yet firmly, told me there were parts of the book that weren't clear, needed to be rewritten, or must be removed. In almost every case they were right.

I am learning to live with questions. I am learning to let go of the need for resolution in all areas of my life before I can be content. There is great peace in not knowing all the answers.

"Be patient toward all that is unresolved in your heart and try to love the questions themselves like locked rooms and like books that are written in a very foreign tongue."—Rainer Maria Rilke

Someone once told me the last thing he let go of had claw marks on it. Perhaps that is a worthy lesson to be learned—yield gracefully, without leaving an imprint.

Be Forgiving

I ALWAYS KNEW THERE WOULD be a section in my book about forgiveness. I never knew I would be blind-sided by my own words, that I would be the one asking to be forgiven.

A few months had gone by since I'd seen the *Merlin* show. I was hard at work on my computer when I felt something trying to get my attention. The cats were sleeping in the other room, their food and water bowls were filled, the stove was off, nothing was on fire . . . exactly *what* was trying to come through?

My mother. It was something about my mother. Something I had done to my mother. Me? What had I done? All things considered, I'd been a pretty good kid. I turned away from the thought and resumed typing.

Oh, no you don't! The thought was persistent.

OK, fine. You've got my attention. Exactly what terrible thing did I do to my mother?

You put your mother through the unspeakable agony of losing her only daughter.

And there it was. The thought that had never crossed my mind, not even once, since my meeting with the shaman eighteen years earlier. He told me I came into my family, into this life, as my older sister, Pamela, but I opted out, knowing the road I would travel in that dysfunctional family would be unbearably painful. At the age of three weeks, I chose death.

To the outside world, I was one more child who had succumbed to SIDS— Sudden Infant Death Syndrome. But from the perspective of reincarnation, I was a terrified soul who put my needs first, without considering the consequences of my actions. I exited this lifetime hoping the cosmic stork would drop me in a much happier family next time around.

Instead, according to the shaman, I was returned to the same family as the next child about two years later. Another girl. Me.

If I believe in reincarnation—that a soul incarnates from one body to another—I also must believe that the soul is responsible for its actions in every lifetime. In other words, karma. If I had deliberately exited my previous life, I was responsible for all the heartache that decision caused.

I lost my mother in 2006, but I'm still close to her two surviving sisters. I called my aunts and asked them how the loss of Pamela had impacted my mother. Each aunt said the same thing—it devastated my mother and took a terrible toll on her marriage.

I found out about Pamela's death when I discovered her birth certificate in Mom's jewelry drawer. I was about ten years old. I don't think I understood what it meant to have a sister who had died. I never really thought about her, because all of my energy was focused on surviving my abusive parents. Now, for the first time since I learned of Pamela, I felt my mother's anguish. I saw her sitting by an empty crib, consumed by her grief, wondering if she had done something to cause her baby's death.

I wondered how this had impacted her young son, Bob— my older brother. Had my mother's torment changed her relationship with him? Had Bob suffered, too? And what about Mom's feelings for me and for the younger brother and sister yet to come? Would the mother/child bond with each of us be skewed by my choice? There was also the question of my father. How had the death of his infant daughter affected him? Is it possible that he grieved, too?

I had spent a large part of my life thinking about forgiveness. Would I ever be able to forgive my father for his horrifying abuse? Could I forgive my mother for the role she played in protecting him? Now that I was looking at forgiveness from the perspective of karma, I had to ask myself if my mother's behavior was any worse than what I had done to her. My heart knew the answer—each of us had deeply wronged the other.

It was time for me to ask my mother for forgiveness. At the exact moment I had that thought, I felt her smiling down on me.

"Already done," Mom said. "And me?"

"Done, Mom."

On September 22, 2012, at 4:00 p.m., I was walking through my bedroom when I suddenly stopped, sat down on the chair, looked up to the heavens, and said, "I forgive you, Dad. This time it's sincere. I hope you've worked through your demons and you're finally at peace."

Who knows—maybe my parents were loving souls who came into this lifetime to help me experience and understand forgiveness. Maybe they were "celestial actors" playing their part in my life's script. I was meant to learn about forgiveness, but I took it upon myself to reject that plan. Perhaps the Universe didn't appreciate the impromptu changes I made to the script, so I was sent back a second time to the same family with the words *Some lessons can't be avoided—this is one of them* written on my cosmic passport.

Note to the Universe: Thank you for your patience. I get it now.

What You Tolerate, You Teach

READ THESE FIVE WORDS. MEMORIZE them. Burn them into your brain. They can make the difference between dragging yourself through a sorrowful life, with bowed head and lowered eyes, or walking through life with joy and purpose, confident the world needs the exceptional gifts that only you can offer.

If we allow others to treat us disrespectfully, we teach them it is acceptable to treat us disrespectfully. It's an easy trap to fall into, especially if you were raised in an abusive home. You learn at an early age that you have little or no value, so you spend your life attracting—and tolerating—people who will reinforce that belief. They may be friends, spouses, family members, employers, or any others who've found their way to you.

With luck, you may reach a point in time when you'll look around and wonder where all the energy vampires who populate your world came from. You'll commit to doing whatever is needed to get your life back on track.

However, if you have been beaten down for years and brainwashed to believe those around you are treating you the way you deserve to be treated, you may spend the rest of your life surrounded by people whose only purpose is to keep you broken. You won't bother trying to escape from the quicksand, because you'll never even know you're in it.

I wish I had understood those words at an earlier age. I didn't. What's important is that I understand them now.

It is *never* too late to reclaim your life.

The act of reclaiming, however, can be unsettling. Taking those first steps back to the magnificent being you are (and always were) can feel like a high-wire act. It's tough to set boundaries with people who've had free rein over you. Some people may easily accept the new, emerging you. Others, however, may push back, believing they still have power over you. They might scream, threaten, cry, or resort to other desperate behaviors to keep you from growing beyond them.

There will be people who fall out of your life, either because they leave on their own or because you find the courage to walk away. Look for those you can rely on to keep you grounded and inspired. If there is no one who can fill this need, consider getting help from a professional. Make a promise to yourself that from this point on, you'll be more discriminating before inviting someone into your inner circle.

Remember these words:

"When people show you who they are, believe them."
—Author and poet Maya Angelou

"When you see crazy coming, cross the street!"
—Speaker and author Iyanla Vanzant

Laugh Often

IN 1996 I WENT BACK to New York City to visit family, eat some pizza, see a Broadway musical, and shop 'till I dropped. I decided to take a side trip to my childhood home, a place I hadn't seen in twenty-three years. I had no idea who lived there now. I wasn't sure if I would actually knock on the door. Perhaps I'd just stand outside. That might be close enough.

It wasn't. I wanted to go up to my bedroom and look around. I was curious to see what my reaction would be. Would I be terrified? Would I scream? Would I sob? Would I feel nothing?

I made my way up the front steps and knocked. The door was opened by a pleasant man, who listened to my story. He remembered my family's name. Of course I could come in. He called to his son, who came downstairs and joined us at the door. The young man looked to be about eighteen years old. His father told him I used to live there and wanted to see the room that had once been mine. The son, who now occupied the room, was agreeable to this, so I followed him up the stairs.

My first thought was how small the room seemed. Had my sister and I really shared this space for so many years? I looked around and my eyes fell on a large poster hanging on the wall. It was a picture of a woman wearing nothing but a few dollops of strategically placed whipped cream . . . and the dollops were melting.

This was what I'd been afraid of?

I wanted to burst out laughing, but somehow that didn't seem like the polite thing to do in front of the room's current occupant. It was obvious this was no longer my room. I sensed nothing terrible within these four walls. The shadows from the past had long been gone. The room belonged to a teenager, and it suited him perfectly.

Over the years, I've tried to remember the son's name, but it's lost somewhere in the gray matter. He did me a great service that day by letting me enter his space. He needed a name. I decided to call him Vinny.

Vinny, wherever you are, and whatever you're doing, I want you to know how grateful I am. You provided exactly what I needed in that moment—comic relief. The last time I left that room I was being secretly moved to Greenwich Village, ready to begin my life in the witness protection program. Thanks to you, I now have closure. I took my final walk out that bedroom door with a light heart and a smile on my face.

They say you should always leave 'em laughing, and Vinny . . . you did.

Part Six

Coming Home

"Home is a name, a word, it is a strong one;
stronger than magician ever spoke,
or spirit ever answered to, in the strongest conjuration."
—Charles Dickens (Martin Chuzzlewit)[19]

A Safe Haven

HOME. IT IS THE MOST beautiful word in the English language. Home is a refuge, a safe haven, a port in the storm. For many people, having a home is taken for granted. They grow up in the home of their parents, where they spend most of their childhood. As they exit their teen years, they move to a college dorm or perhaps to a first apartment. Their next residence likely comes with a mortgage. Each of these locations gives them a sense of place; there is a dot on a map, with four walls and a roof, and that's where they belong.

For other people, such as myself, having a home seemed like a dream. Maybe, someday, I would stumble upon the enchanted forest where all the happy homes lived, where one would instantly recognize me as the person who was meant to carry its key. A path to the home would run up to my feet, and as I walked through the front door, I would know I had found the place where I was meant to be.

I spent my entire life looking for my home. I thought it would be a building of wood, shingles, and glass. Over time, I began to believe my home would be a place within me, a sanctuary in my heart that would always be there, no matter where my feet were planted. Now I know that, given all the grief I carried, I was going to have a difficult time finding my true home, whether in my outer world or my inner world.

For one thing, there was that little issue of being disconnected from my body. What four walls could have contained such a spectral presence? Then there was my hidden rage. How could I ever have found my safe haven when something so unsafe was lurking within me? I may not have been conscious of it, but some part of my psyche would have wanted that unwelcome guest on the other side of the front door.

Had I known about my unresolved rage, I might have felt comfortable inviting it into my home, hoping that one day we would do the work leading to its release. But without recognizing—and claiming—my anger, I suspect its dark presence made it impossible for any home to open its arms to me.

Interior designer, Nate Berkus, says your home should rise up to greet you. Mine was running as fast as it could in the opposite direction.

Why Arthur?

ALL THAT CHANGED IN THE summer of 2012, when a prince from another world found a way to touch my heart with magic. I have no doubt the extraordinary events of that night were divinely inspired. The unanswered question is why did this divine inspiration move through Arthur Pendragon of Camelot? Why was he chosen as the messenger to deliver me from a heartbreaking past and put me on a path to peace and wholeness?

Perhaps the answer was in front of me all along. I fell in love with the story of Camelot when I was very young, desperately trying to survive my father's abuse. I learned of its great king, Arthur. He was a man of honor, good and true. Seen through the eyes of a little girl, he was the knight in shining armor riding bravely into battle, fighting for what was right. He held up his sword for those who were in peril. I had already withdrawn into my imagination and was living in a dream world, hoping that one day I would be released from my suffering. I had gone to my mother for help, and she turned away from me. Is it so hard to imagine that to this lost child, Arthur would be the one and only person who could save her from her father?

When I spoke with Dr. William Miller about his book, *Quantum Change: When Epiphanies and Sudden Insights Transform Ordinary Lives*,[20] the first question I asked him was how could I have been unaware of the terrifying rage that had been buried inside me since I was a child?

He told me the brain has a remarkable ability to compartmentalize when dealing with trauma. As a seven-year-old girl, I had no way of reconciling the anger I felt for my father, so I locked it away in a dark chamber within my brain. It would always be there, but I would have no knowledge of it.

Since the brain has the ability to keep parts of our past hidden from us, was the idea of Arthur coming to my rescue something else I locked away in my brain? Would Arthur remain hidden unless—or until—a specific set of circumstances, far into the future, were set in motion? Was this why the extraction of my rage was facilitated by a character I trusted from childhood, who would bring me triumphantly through the fire and leave me standing my ground?

This seems like a plausible explanation for why my liberation from the past would only occur with the intervention of Arthur. It satisfies both my brain and my soul. I can find no loose ends—except one.

I will always wonder what happened in the moment just before I began screaming in my bedroom, when Arthur confronted his father on the television screen. How did I get off my bed and arrive at the other side of my room? There is a gap in my memory that intrigues me. I suppose the answer could be simple—I stood up, walked around my four-poster bed, and stopped in front of the TV.

But another solution has been tugging at my heart since the beginning of this journey. What if the divine presence that gifted me with this miracle knew I would be overwhelmed by the events about to come? I had unknowingly granted my rage safe harbor within my body. Would I try to protect it, like a mother bear defending her cub? After all, I didn't willingly give the anger up. It was forcibly removed from me.

What if a bridge was built through the heavens, connecting me with a television show created three years earlier? What if the knight from my childhood walked over that bridge to deliver a message of comfort and reassurance? Perhaps he stood at the end of my bed and whispered, "Don't be afraid. I'm the one you met in your dreams when you were a little girl. I've come to pull the sorrow from your heart, just as I once pulled a sword from a stone. You trusted me once—trust me again. You won't remember these words, and that is as it should be. All you need to do is surrender."

And surrender, I did.

Home at Last

MY QUANTUM CHANGE GAVE ME many gifts. Making peace with my past was just the beginning. I am essentially pain free, a gift worth its weight in gold. Maintaining the thirty-pound weight loss has been easy, because I recognize when I'm actually hungry and how much food I require. My heart and soul are fully integrated with my body. This continues to be one of the most delicious parts of my extraordinary year.

The rewiring of my brain remains in place. Now that I understand how the brain works, I pay close attention to what I'm thinking. My sword—Clarity—delights, uplifts, and challenges me each and every day. She is mouthy and stubborn, just two of the many traits I love about her.

So many gifts . . . and yet one more. As the end of my journey was in sight, I realized I had arrived at an unexpected threshold. I didn't have to use my key—the door opened all on its own. I looked behind me and took one last glance at the road I had traveled for the past twelve months. The people who joined me on my adventure were there to wave me on.

I turned and walked into the entryway. Light spilled through the many windows and set the walls aglow. My books and paints and music filled the welcoming rooms. Molly, true to her feline nature, napped in a patch of sunlight by the hearth. Star, who left her earthly life just before my journey ended, watched over us from afar as she soared among the constellations. Clarity rested on my desk, ready to be of service. There was no sorrow here. No hidden monsters. I felt only peace. And that is exactly how it should feel, when you finally come home.

Watership Down

MY FAVORITE BOOK OF ALL time is *Watership Down*,[21] by Richard Adams. It is a fantasy about a band of rabbits, who are forced to leave their warren when man intrudes upon their idyllic life and brings destruction to these peaceful creatures. The rabbits set out to find a new grassy hillside in the English Downs, where they can build their tunnels and raise their young.

I have read this book more times than I can count. I eagerly follow Hazel, the chief rabbit, and his brother, Fiver, the visionary who provides guidance for their perilous journey. I lose my heart to Bigwig every time I travel with these brave adventurers. He is the warrior and my favorite of the rabbits.

Watership Down is a teaching story. For me, the most important lesson is that every rabbit, even those who seem insignificant or frivolous, has a purpose. Each one plays an important part in their survival.

My story of the past year often paralleled that of the rabbits. Like them, my travels provided moments of great joy, extraordinary clarity, and heartbreaking despair. I made new friends along the way, just as the rabbits did, while old friends returned when they were desperately needed. When the time came to confront our opponents, both the rabbits and I came to a fork in the road. We faced the same choices: we could remain separate from our adversaries and move toward destruction with fear and anger in our hearts, or we could step beyond our histories and face the future together.

I chose to make peace with my past and with all the characters who had played their parts in my life. And how did the rabbits fare? You'll just have to read *Watership Down* to see how their adventure comes to a close.

As for my story, I realized I'd spent too many years seeking that which I thought was missing from my life. In the end, I learned it wasn't a matter of finding something that was lost, but rather removing the obstacle that had kept it hidden. Nowhere was that more evident than in my search for a home. It had been there all along, beneath my rage. Once that rage was gone, my safe haven appeared—just like magic! I wondered if this was how Dorothy felt when she learned she could have gone home whenever she wanted to. All she had to do was click her heels together three times. So simple, once you know how.

Epilogue

"We'll be friends until forever, just you wait and see."

—A.A. Milne

I SUPPOSE I WILL ALWAYS spend a lot of time in my imagination. That's one habit I could never break—not that I would want to. In the space between my imagination and my dreams, I see myself living on a high, grassy hill in the English Downs. There are large trees on this hill that send their massive roots into the ground. The thick roots make sturdy rooftops for the underground rabbit warrens and keep the tunnels free from rain. My home lives at the top of the hill. From there I can see far out over the countryside, a vantage point that alerts me of predators the rabbits should know about. (Rabbits are particularly vulnerable to stoats and foxes.)

Beyond the downs sits a castle. There is always much activity there— knights coming and going on horseback, jousters thrilling spectators in the arena, magicians juggling planets pulled from the sky.

Each month, on the night of the full moon, I wander down the hillside and stop beneath a large beech tree. A cavernous hole has been dug at its base. It is a burrow spacious enough to fit three friends who meet regularly for tea and tales—a gift from the many rabbits who worked to excavate it. The ground in this over-sized burrow is lined with fur, pulled by the mother rabbits from their bellies. That is how they've kept their babies warm throughout time. This hole, however, is not for the rabbits . . . save one.

When I arrive, Bigwig is waiting for me. The torn ears from his final battle make me weep, as always. He gently touches my arm with his paw and guides me down the hole. We take our places within the gnarled roots that wind their way into the earth. Clarity rests by my side, content within the fur. An owl hoots softly in the distance.

Then we hear footsteps. We look up and see his silhouette in the entrance, lit by an autumn moon. He makes his way down the opening, stepping into the tapestry of twisted roots. The red cape swings behind him as he settles to the ground, laying his sword next to Clarity. He is older now, but I still see a hint of the young man who found me all those years ago and sent me on the most extraordinary journey of my life.

We sit before a circle of wood, hewn from a fallen tree trunk. It is our round table. Often we tell stories of the battles we've fought over the ages. Sometimes we dream of a future where knights and rabbits and little girls can live in peace. Tonight, however, is not a time for tales. It is a time for remembrance.

Fifty years ago today, a prince from a faraway kingdom stepped through a portal in time and space and breathed fire into the dying embers of my soul. He healed that which I did not know was broken. What was no longer needed exploded into nothingness. I should have been decimated in the blast, but I wasn't. Instead, I held my ground.

I was left standing in a cool mist. It touched my cheeks and mingled with my tears. The prince stood before me, holding a sword. A soft light danced around the edges of the blade. Moss grew on the stars that embellished the cross-guard. Dirt and pine needles were embedded in the spiral pommel. The prince placed the blade in my hands. I knew this sword! I had held it before, far away from this hillside. "Yes," he said. "She, too, has come home." Then he smiled, and took a step toward me. He leaned in close and whispered five extraordinary words. Just five words, but they would change the rest of my life and all the lives yet to come.

Slowly we emerge from our memories. Bigwig offers to pour the tea and he reaches for my cup. We sit in silence, the three of us—the man, the woman, and the rabbit. We are thankful for the quiet. It is like that among old friends.

Notes

Part One

1. R. A. Salvatore, *Streams of Silver*. (Seattle: Wizards of the Coast, 1989).

2. William R. Miller and Janet C'de Baca, *Quantum Change: When Epiphanies and Sudden Insights Transform Ordinary Lives*. (New York: The Guilford Press, 2001).

3. *The Sins of the Father*, Merlin, (c) Shine TV 2009

4. Ibid.

5. Ibid.

6. Ibid.

7. Sandra Ingerman, *Soul Retrieval: Mending the Fragmented Self*. (San Francisco: HarperSanFrancisco, 1991).

8. Clarissa Pinkola Estés, *Women Who Run with the Wolves* (Audiobook). (Sounds True Audio, 1990).

Part Two

9. Elaine Aron, *The Highly Sensitive Person*. (New York: Carol Publishing Group, 1996).

10. Andrea Bartz, "Sense and Sensitivity". *(Psychology Today*, July 5, 2011).

Part Three

11. Wayne W. Dyer, *Secrets of Manifesting* (Live Lecture Recording). (Hay House, Inc., 2012).

12. William R. Miller and Janet C'de Baca, *Quantum Change: When Epiphanies and Sudden Insights Transform Ordinary Lives*. (New York: The Guilford Press, 2001).

13. William R. Miller and Janet C'de Baca, *Quantum Change: When Epiphanies and Sudden Insights Transform Ordinary Lives.* (New York: The Guilford Press, 2001, p.181).

14. Deepak Chopra, *The Return of Merlin.* (New York: Harmony Books, 1995).

15. Bronnie Ware, *The Top Five Regrets of the Dying.* (Hay House, Inc., 2012).

Part Four

16. Dr. Seuss, *Oh, the Places You'll Go.* (New York: Random House, 1990).

17. Sharon Begley, *Train Your Mind Change Your Brain.* (New York: Ballantine Books, 2007).

Part Five

18. Richard Bach, *Illusions.* (UK: Arrow Books Ltd., 2001).

Part Six

19. Charles Dickens, *Martin Chuzzlewit.* (UK: Wordsworth Editions Ltd., 1998).

20. William R. Miller and Janet C'de Baca, *Quantum Change: When Epiphanies and Sudden Insights Transform Ordinary Lives.* (New York: The Guilford Press, 2001).

21. Richard Adams, *Watership Down.* (London: Rex Collings Ltd., 1972).

We hope you enjoyed this Lighthearted Press book. To
order additional copies, please contact your local bookstore
or visit us online at www.lightheartedpress.com.

Books by Christine Davis:

Breathing Fire
Forever Paws
For Every Dog An Angel
For Every Cat An Angel
The Shelter Dog
Old Dog and the Christmas Wish

Lighthearted Press Inc.
P.O. Box 90125
Portland, OR 97290
503-786-3085 (phone)
503-786-0315 (fax)
877-385-6837 (toll free)
www.lightheartedpress.com